T UIDE

TASMANIA

A TRAVELLING COMPANION

CONTENTS

ISBN 0 949457 32 9

Published and distributed by
Regal Publications
24 Wellington Street, Launceston
Tasmania 7250

Telephone: (03) 6331 4222
Facsimile: (03) 6331 4904

Nearly all the drawings in this book can be coloured-in. To help you with the animals, plants and birds, there are descriptions nearby.

THE FIRST TASMANIANS

Most of the early explorers found the Tasmanian Aborigines cheerful and friendly. However, when white settlement began all that changed. In 1803, Lieutenant Bowen began a settlement at Risdon Cove, near where the bridge named after him, crosses the Derwent River today. A group of about 500 aborigines gathered on the hill above the camp. Whether they were hostile or just curious, we'll never know. Soldiers were ordered to open fire and about 50 were shot and killed. From then on hatred and mistrust between the new settlers and the original inhabitants grew.

At that time there were about four thousand aborigines living around Tasmania except in the wet and mountainous areas of the west and south. They lived in groups of between 40 to 50 people which consisted of families who each had their own shelter and fire.

They moved about hunting, gathering edible plants, shellfish and lobsters. With them, they carried a lighted stick. With these firesticks they lit fires for cooking and warmth but they were also used to "farm" the land. As they moved from camp to camp they would set fire to special areas of land. This "farming" encouraged the growth of native grasses which attracted grazing animals as well as making travelling much easier.

With spears and clubs they hunted wallabies, possums, kangaroos, echidnas and wombats. By the sea they also visited islands and rocks to kill seals. To get out to the islands they made canoes by tying bundles of bark together with reeds.

They built shelters which ranged from simple windbreaks made out of bark leaning against a branch to woven, dome shaped huts that were lined with feathers and could hold up to fifteen people.

They wore very little clothing. The women wore a kangaroo skin mainly for carrying items such as digging sticks, scraper stones and clubs. The children were naked and men only occasionally wore skin cloaks. They covered themselves with a mixture of fat, ochre and charcoal which not only helped keep out the cold and wet but also deterred biting insects. They wore necklaces of shells, leather and bone and scarred their skin in patterns. Hairstyles were very varied. Some had their heads totally shaved while others, especially men, had elaborate hairstyles matted with mud and ochre.

In the first seventy years of European settlement the aboriginies were hunted, shot and poisoned. Some fought back and some white settlers were killed but spears and clubs are not much of a match against pistols and guns.

Not all of the white settlers treated the aborigines badly and the government made attempts to re-settle the remaining aborigines in reserves. Unfortunately, due to diseases introduced by the white settlers, poor food, despair and homesickness they too died. By 1876, Truganinni, the last full-blooded Tasmanian Aboriginal had died.

Today there are about one thousand Aboriginal people living in Tasmania and on the surrounding islands. They are the descendants of Aboriginal women and the sealers who kidnapped them in the early days of white settlement.

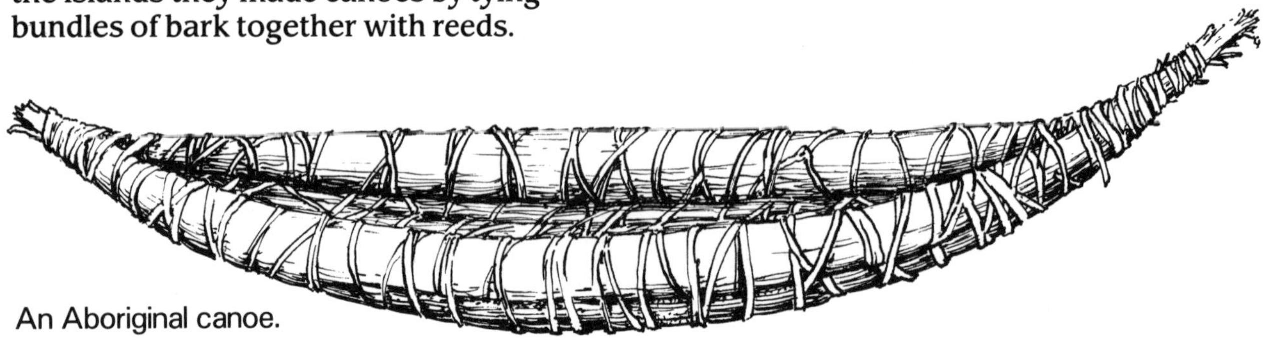

An Aboriginal canoe.

No Boomerangs! Did you know Tasmanian Aborigines never used boomerangs. They were first used by Mainland Aborigines about ten thousand years ago. By then the ice caps and glaciers of the last Ice Age had melted and Tasmania was cut-off from the rest of Australia by rising seas which formed Bass Strait.

If you want to find out more about the First Tasmanians visit Tiagarra Aboriginal Centre at Devonport's Mersey Bluff. On the bluff itself you can see Aboriginal rock carvings. Other places to visit include the Queen Victoria Museum and Art Gallery in Launceston or the Tasmanian Museum and Art Gallery in Hobart.

In 1828, Governor Arthur had this poster nailed to trees in the bush. He was trying to get a message across to the Aborigines who did not read and the white settlers, most of whom, could not read.

What do you think he was trying to say with these pictures?

A windbreak shelter.

A dome hut built by tribes along the west and south coasts.

Here are some Aboriginal words that have been given to places in Tasmania.

CETHANA — Hair
KOONYA — Swan
LENAH — Brush Kangaroo
LIAPOOTHAH — Creek
LIAWENEE — Fresh Water
MARRAWAH — One

MAYDENA — Shadow
MOONAH — Gum Tree
NUBEENA — Crayfish
PARATTAH — Frost or Hail
POATINA — Cave
TAROONA — Chiton (Shellfish)

If you go for a walk on the beach, keep a lookout for piles of old shells. These mounds, called MIDDENS, are the remains of the shellfish eaten by Aborigines over the centuries.

EARLY EUROPEAN EXPLORERS

Abel Tasman

George Bass

ABEL TASMAN

One hundred and thirty eight years before Captain Cook came to Australia a man named Captain Abel Willem Janzoon Tasman had sailed around the southern half of the Tasmanian Coastline. On November the 24th, 1642, Tasman and his men became the first Europeans to set foot on Tasmania which they named Van Diemen's Land. They sailed around the coastline for eleven days and gathered wood and water here.

Tasman had been sent by Anthony Van Diemen for two reasons. Firstly, to find a new route to South America and secondly to look for new riches such as gold or spices.

Tasman's ships had difficulty sailing up the east coast of Van Diemen's Land and so he departed.

A few days later, he "bumped" into another island. The name he gave it, is still used today — NEW ZEALAND.

BASS AND FLINDERS

George Bass was a naval surgeon who was also a keen natural scientist. He was so keen that he brought a small boat with him from England, the "Tom Thumb." On the voyage to Australia he became friends with Matthew Flinders who had been to Australia before with Captain William Bligh.

Together, in their free time, Bass and Flinders explored and mapped the coast around Sydney.

Bass, like many people of the time, believed Van Diemen's Land (Tasmania) might actually be an island. In a slightly larger boat "Tom Thumb II" he set sail alone and arrived at Westernport near where Melbourne is today. If he could prove Van Diemen's Land was an island it would cut 3 weeks off the dangerous voyage between England and Sydney.

Eventually Governor Hunter provided Bass and Flinders with a small ship, the "Norfolk", a crew of ten and supplies.

In 1798 they became the first people to circumnavigate (travel around) Tasmania. They mapped and named many features. The Governor was so pleased that they had proved a strait existed that he named it Bass's Strait.

Tasmania wasn't always called Tasmania. Until 1855 it was called Van Diemen's Land.

After their voyage of discovery the two men went their separate ways. Bass became a partner in a trading company. In 1803 he sailed from Sydney in the company's ship "Venus".

The ship, the crew and George Bass were never seen again!

Matthew Flinders, between 1801-1803, became the first person to circumnavigate the whole of Australia. He invented a special method for correcting marine compasses and to this very day there are Flinders Bars on the boxes which house ships' compasses.

Many places and things in Tasmania are named after Bass and Flinders, how many can you spot? Are you circumnavigating Tasmania by road?

Matthew Flinders

Use this space to jot down some of the things named after Tasman, Bass and Flinders.

The French explored many parts of Southern and Eastern Tasmania before it was settled. That is why many places along the east coast have French names. The explorers were Marion Du Fresne, La Perouse, Bruny D'Entrecastreaux, and Huon De Kermadec.

THE SYDNEY TO HOBART YACHT RACE

The Sydney to Hobart race is rated by sailors as the most exciting and dangerous yacht race in the world.

It began in 1945 with only 8 yachts. Every Boxing Day, since then, sailors cross the starting line in Sydney. Today, with over 120 yachts competing, the organisers use two starting lines to avoid collisions!

After leaving Sydney Harbour the boats turn South and depending on the weather usually cross the finish line in Hobart a few days later. The record for the fastest time set was 1 day, 19 hours and 45 minutes. The slowest was "Wayfarer" which took over 11 days!

If you are in Hobart around New Year's Day then join in the excitement and visit the yachts tied up at Constitution Dock.

CONVICTS

On the 26th January 1788, (the day Australia now celebrates as it's birthday), 750 convicts landed at Sydney Cove. For the next eighty-nine years until Transportation stopped in 1877 the British Government sent prisoners to the colony of Australia. They were sent for crimes ranging from such minor offences as stealing a loaf of bread to murder. The voyage out was cramped and dangerous. Many died on the way.

In Tasmania the first convicts arrived with free settlers as well as soldiers. They provided free labour which helped establish towns and industries such as timbercutting and boat building. It was probably quite a privilege to be included in these first work parties. The government wanted the settlements in Tasmania to succeed so their food and working conditions were better.

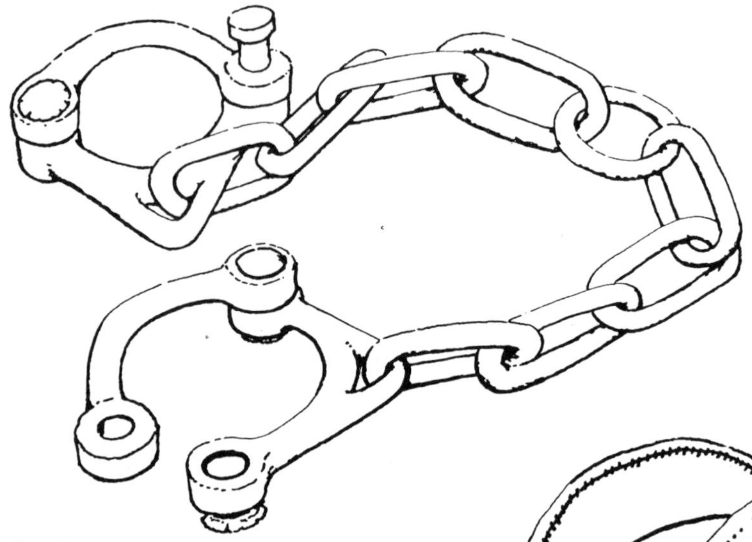

Leg irons.
These ones weighed 7 kilograms!

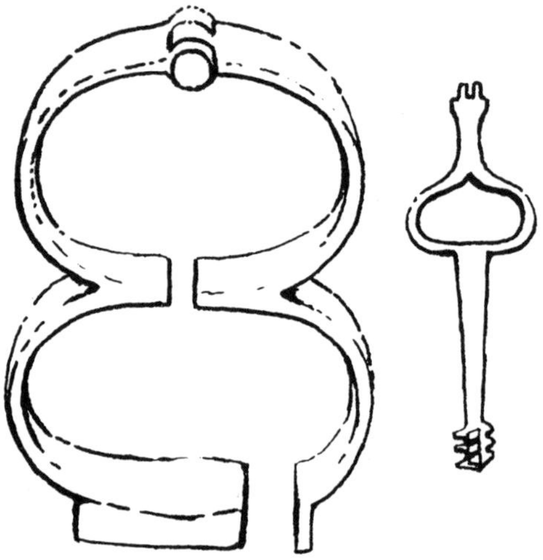

Convict handcuff and key

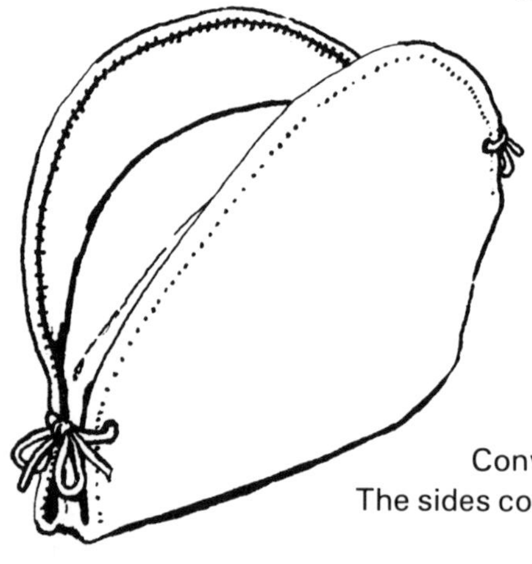

Convict leather cap.
The sides could be turned down in bad weather.

Eventually however, Van Diemen's Land, as it was called then, became the most feared and hated of all penal colonies. The first of the dreaded prisons was built at Macquarie Harbour on the wild west coast. Governor Macquarie, in New South Wales, decided that a place was needed to separate and punish the most troublesome convicts. Those sent to Macquarie Harbour were never expected to leave it!

The work was unbelievably hard. In the thickest, darkest and wettest forests of Australia they worked from sunrise to sunset cutting Huon Pine trees for boatbuilding. Most of the time they wore heavy chains and were fed only two meals a day. One of the 'meals' was flour mixed with water! Within eleven years 85 prisoners had died and of the 112 convicts who had escaped into the bush 62 had died and nine had been murdered by fellow escapees for food!

The other infamous prison was at Port Arthur. At first Port Arthur was used as a timber camp as well but the convicts who worked there were skilled men and were treated well.

After a mutiny at Macquarie Harbour, Governor Arthur decided to build a large prison nearer to Hobart Town. He chose Port Arthur. It was surrounded by water except for a very narrow strip of land. That strip is called Eaglehawk Neck and on it were placed a row of savage dogs.

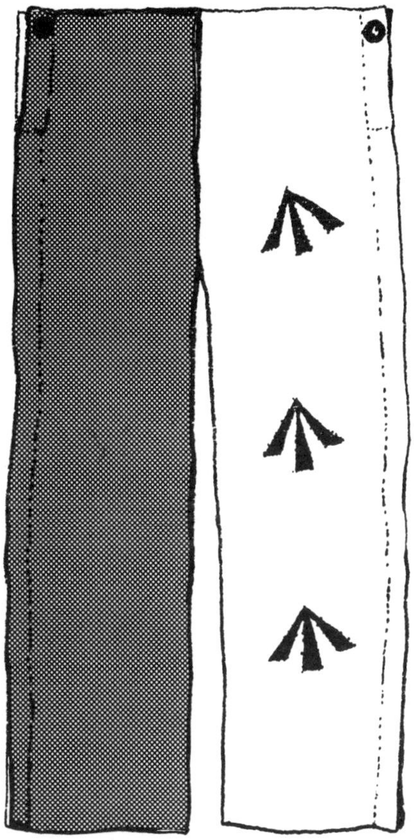

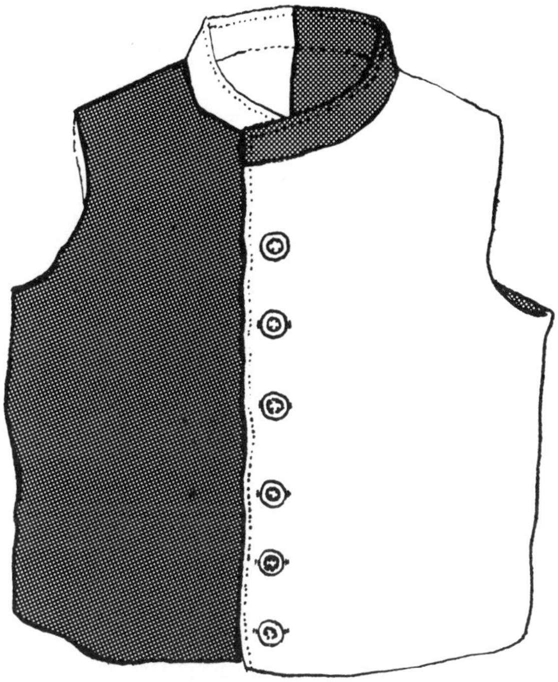

Heavy woollen jacket and pants. Convicts who were re-sentenced wore these black and yellow outfits. The pants unbuttoned up the sides so that the leg-irons were not removed.

YOUNG BOYS WERE IMPRISONED AT PORT ARTHUR TOO. IN 1844 THERE WERE NEARLY 700.

Convicts weren't just kept in prisons though. The 'well behaved' ones were hired out to farmers and builders. Others worked on road gangs. Without convict labour the early settlements may never have survived let alone grown and prospered.

Many convicts when their sentences were over chose to stay and make a new life in Australia rather than be returned penniless to the crowded slums of Britain.

Wherever you go in Tasmania today you can see the results of the convicts' labours. Many of the buildings and bridges they made are still in use today.

To get a better idea of how the convicts lived you could visit Port Arthur, Richmond Gaol, catch a ferry to Sarah Island on Macquarie Harbour or go to the museums in Hobart or Launceston.

Tasmania's first train featured an ''engine'' of four convicts!

TASMANIAN NATIVE ANIMALS

POTOROO

Colour: Brown to Grey lighter underneath, Nose; pink
Size: Head to Tail 53cm to 63cm
Distribution: Open forest & scrub North & East Tasmania.
Food: Roots, tubers, fungi, insects and worms.
Notes: The Potoroo runs rather than hops and is smaller than the Bettong. It builds a nest of grass which it sleeps in during the day. Also found in parts of South-East Australia.

BETTONG

Colour: Browny Grey, white underneath. Tail tipped with white.
Size: **Head to tail: 60cm to 70cm.**
Distribution: Grassy areas throughout Tasmania except West Coast.
Food: Fungi, seeds, roots and bulbs.
Notes: Builds a woven nest of grasses, usually under a log, which it sleeps in during the day. Unlike the smaller Potoroo, Bettong hop along. Now extinct on the mainland because of foxes and competition for food from rabbits.

Nocturnal means an animal sleeps during the day and is awake at night.

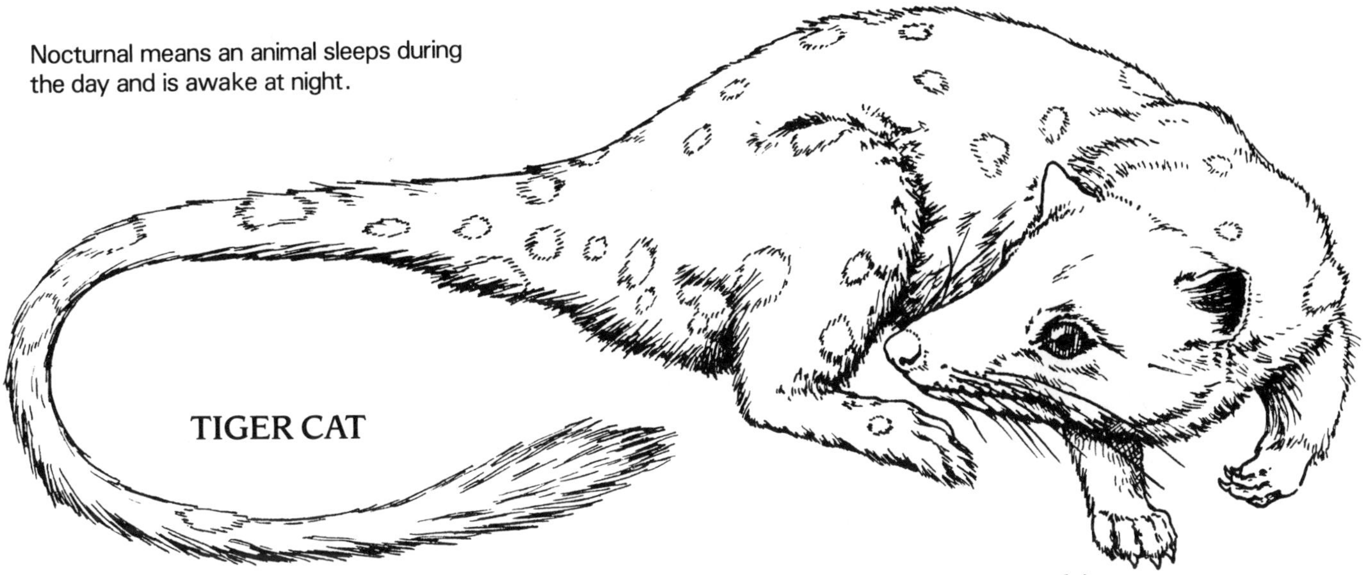

TIGER CAT

Colour: Body and Tail; orange-brown with white spots, Belly; yellow-white.
Size: Head to Tail; 70cm to 1.4m.
Distribution: Throughout Tasmania.
Food: Small animals and birds.
Notes: It can climb but spends most of its time on the forest floor. Nests in caves and hollows in trees and logs. It is mainly nocturnal but sometimes hunts and basks in the sun during the day. The Tiger Cat is also found in South-East Australia.

NATIVE CAT

Colour: Black to brown-grey with white spots on body only, Belly; white, Nose and Ears; pink.
Size: Head to Tail; 44cm to 73cm.
Distribution: Throughout Tasmania.
Food: Insects, rats, carcasses of dead animals, grasses and berries.
Notes: The Native Cat is smaller than the Tiger Cat. The young Native Cats are reared in a grass-lined den and are very playful and can be seen in clearings around sunset chasing each other's tails just like domestic kittens. The Native Cat was seen in South-Eastern Australia but is now thought to be extinct there.

If you are camping or spending a night in the countryside and hear thumping, screeching and hissing noises, don't be scared, those sounds are probably just possums. Grab a torch and watch them.

As well as Ringtail and Brush Possums, Tasmania also has Sugar Gliders (possums that glide) and two types of tiny possums known as Pygmy Possums.

PADEMELON OR RUFOUS WALLABY

Colour:	Dark brown with reddish tinge, feet; black.
Size:	Head to tail; 88cm to 1.1 metres.
Distribution:	Throughout Tasmania where areas of grass meet forest.
Food:	Grass and herbs.
Notes:	One of only two wallabies found in Tasmania, it was once found in Victoria but is now extinct there. Easily distinguished from the Bennett's wallaby because it is much smaller and has a short tail.

BENNETT'S WALLABY

Colour:	Reddish grey to light grey underneath.
Size:	1.3m to 1.8m.
Distribution:	Throughout Tasmania.
Food:	Grass and herbs.
Notes:	Also found on the East Coast of the mainland. Often seen during the day. If you want to pat one then visit Waldheim at Cradle Mountain.

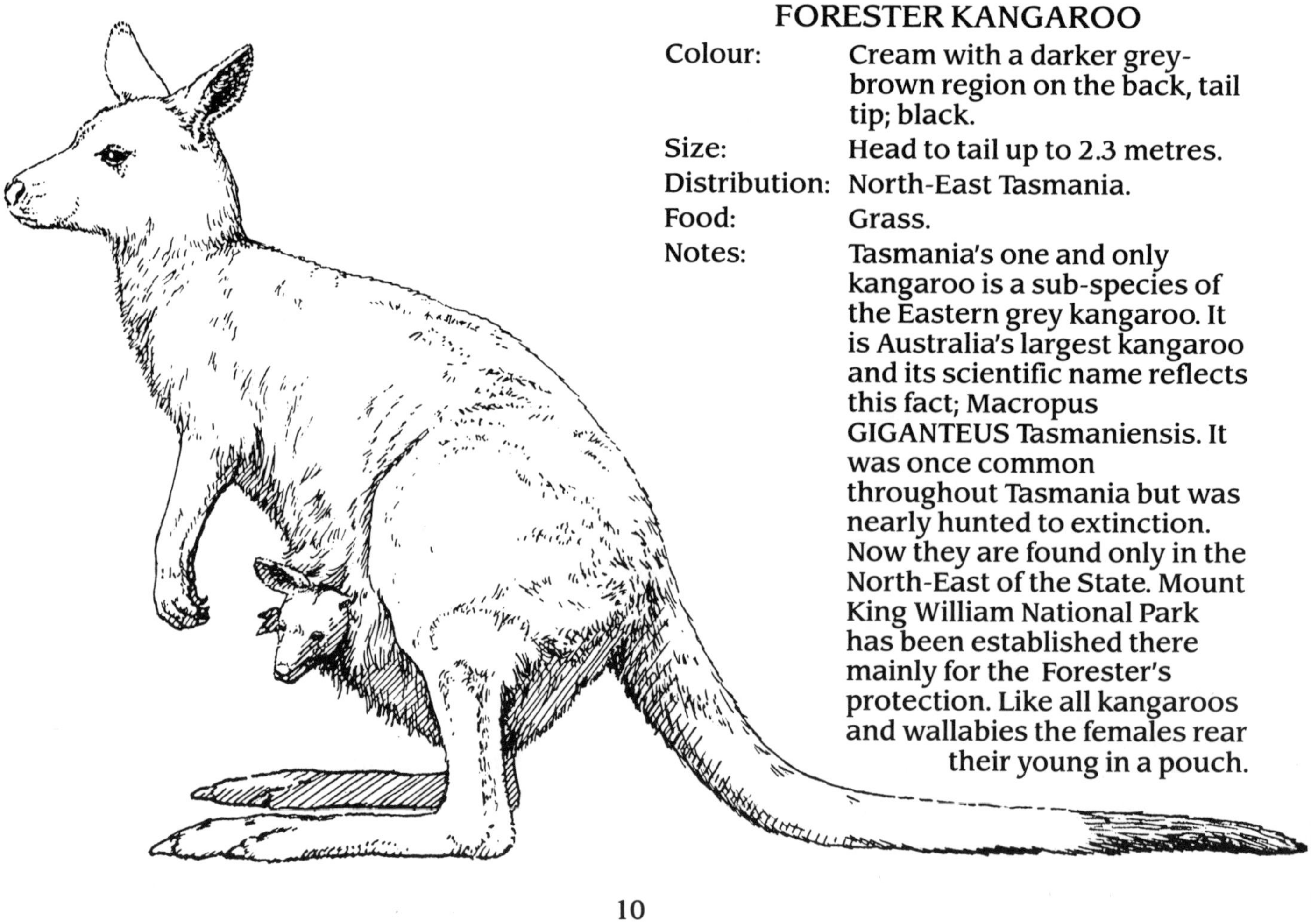

FORESTER KANGAROO

Colour:	Cream with a darker grey-brown region on the back, tail tip; black.
Size:	Head to tail up to 2.3 metres.
Distribution:	North-East Tasmania.
Food:	Grass.
Notes:	Tasmania's one and only kangaroo is a sub-species of the Eastern grey kangaroo. It is Australia's largest kangaroo and its scientific name reflects this fact; Macropus GIGANTEUS Tasmaniensis. It was once common throughout Tasmania but was nearly hunted to extinction. Now they are found only in the North-East of the State. Mount King William National Park has been established there mainly for the Forester's protection. Like all kangaroos and wallabies the females rear their young in a pouch.

Brushtail Possum with baby.

POSSUMS

BRUSH POSSUM

Colour:	Black to reddish-brown or grey, tail; black, nose; pink.
Size:	Head to tail, 74cm to 92cm.
Distribution:	Throughout Tasmania.
Food:	Leaves, fruit, buds, bark and pasture grasses.
Notes:	The Brush Possum is nocturnal but unlike the ringtail it does not build nests. It will sleep in any place that is dark and enclosed. It is more common in the wetter parts of the State. Its soft thick fur is exported worldwide.

Ringtail Possum

RINGTAIL POSSUM

Colour:	Creamy grey to dark brown. Tail tip; white, nose and ears; pink.
Size:	Head to tail, 60cm to 70cm.
Distribution:	Throughout Tasmania.
Food:	Leaves, fruit and flowers.
Notes:	The Ringtail is nocturnal and spends the day sleeping in tree hollows or a ball-shaped nest made out of sticks and twigs. It is more common in the drier eastern half of the State. Common in Eastern Australia.

PLATYPUS

Colour: Nose or Beak and Feet; black, Back and Tail; brown, Belly; light grey

Size: Approximately 50 cm. Males larger than Females.

Distribution: Lakes, rivers and streams throughout Tasmania except near the larger towns and cities.

Food: Water insects, molluscs, small crustaceans and worms.

Notes: The Platypus lives in a burrow which it digs beneath the shore of a lake or river. The entrance is below the water level and the tunnel slopes upwards, sometimes as far as fifty feet. The female lays from one to three eggs in a special chamber lined with grass and leaves. The sensitive beak is used to forage about on the riverbed.

ECHIDNA

Colour: Back; dark brown, Head and Belly; light brown, Nose; black, Spines; brown and white.

Size: Approximately 40 cm.

Distribution: Common in several parts of Tasmania especially the lakes district and the North and East Coasts.

Food: Ants and their eggs.

Notes: The Echidna is amazingly strong for its size. If it senses danger it will burrow very quickly. The claws and spines do not contain poison as many people once believed. It has a long skinny tongue coated in sticky saliva to lap up the ants it feeds on.

> MONOTREMES The Platypus and Echidna are the world's only egg-laying mammals. Because of this they are both known as Monotremes.

WOMBAT

Colour: Brown, Nose; black.
Size: 90cm to 1 metre.
Distribution: Throughout Tasmania.
Food: Grass and roots.
Notes: Wombats are mainly nocturnal but during the cold months or after snowfalls often feed during the day. They live in large burrows often up to a dozen some of which may be as long as 20 metres. The female wombat has a pouch which faces backwards to stop dirt from entering it.

TASMANIAN DEVIL

Colour: Black with white patches. Nose; pink.
Size: Approx. 70 to 80cm.
Distribution: Only found in Tasmania. Common throughout except in towns and cities.
Food: Any dead or decaying animals, also birds or hens.
Notes: The Devil is strictly nocturnal. It has very powerful jaws and eats the bones,as well as the flesh,of carcasses (dead bodies) it finds. The devil used to eat the Tasmanian Tiger's leftovers. Sometimes more than one devil will feed on a carcass which often leads to noisy arguments of growls and screams.

SNAKES

TIGER SNAKE

Colour: Black to golden-brown often slightly striped.
Length: 90cm to 150cm.
Distribution: Common throughout Tasmania.

Copperhead Snake

Tiger Snake

COPPERHEAD SNAKE

Colour: Black to Reddish Brown.
Length: 90cm to 150cm.
Distribution: Common throughout Tasmania mainly near marshes and swamps.

Whipsnake

WHIPSNAKE

Colour: Extremely variable: most commonly bronze or sage green - white lips.
Length: 50cm.
Distribution: All over. Most commonly seen in Alpine areas.

SNAKES

THE BAD NEWS: There are three types of snake found in Tasmania and they are all poisonous. Do NOT pester or poke them.
THE GOOD NEWS: Snakes hibernate in the cooler months and are usually only seen from October to March.

THE MIGHTY LITTLE MUTTONBIRD

Every September over 16 million Muttonbirds arrive on the coast and islands of Tasmania. They have just completed a journey of at least 30,000 kilometres!

If they can they will return to exactly the same burrow. They spend their first few weeks here squabbling, courting and fixing up burrows or digging new ones.

Almost straight away the adult females lay one egg each. For about 53 days the "parents" take it in turns to sit on the egg and keep it warm.

Two days after the egg hatches the young bird is left alone in the burrow during the day. The adult birds have gone off to sea in search of food, which is mostly krill. They take it in turns to return just after sunset and feed the chick. After about three months the baby bird is bigger than its parents, weighing just over a kilogram.

By mid April the adults take off again on their long flight which will take them to Alaska and back. The young birds leave a couple of weeks later.

In the early days of settlement in Tasmania, Muttonbirds were hunted heavily and their numbers began to decline.

Today the birds are protected by law and the people who harvest them must have a licence. In March every year about 160,000 young birds are taken but their population is slowly growing again.

The flesh which is salted and sold as food was the reason why the early settlers called them Muttonbirds. Other products from the Muttonbird are fat, oil and feathers, If you have a down-filled sleeping bag then it probably contains Muttonbird feathers.

Matthew Flinders in 1798 wrote this description of Muttonbirds in his diary.

> "There was a stream, fifty to eighty yards in depth and three hundred yards in breadth; the birds were flying compactly and during a full hour and a half continued to pass without interruption."
>
> Can you imagine that many birds? Flinders guessed there were over 150 million just in that one flock.

MUTTON BIRD or SHORT-TAILED SHEARWATER

Colour: Sooty brown body and wings. Light grey throat and belly. Grey beak. Purple-grey legs and feet.

THE JET SETTING MUTTONBIRDS

Muttonbirds fly north for winter. Join the dots and find out where they go.

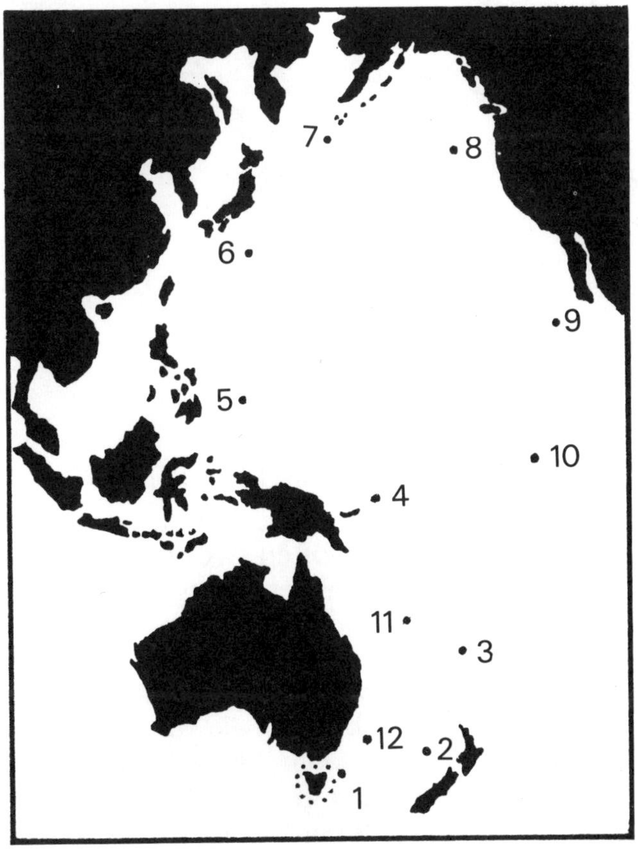

BIRDS

There are at least 265 different birds that live in or visit Tasmania. Obviously I can't show them all in this book. I have shown some of the birds you are most likely to see in Tasmania. All of them can be coloured in.

Many birds, such as the Muttonbird, migrate to Tasmania during the warmer months. Some birds, like the Starling and Sparrow, were introduced by early settlers. Of all these birds, only 12 are native to Tasmania. Happy bird-watching.

TASMANIAN NATIVE HEN

The Native Hen doesn't look like the Road-runner on the Bugs Bunny Show but it behaves like it. It never flies and is often seen running across paddocks at quite a high speed. Like the Swamphen it's tail flicks as it walks. It eats grasses, seeds and insects.

Voice: A harsh "see-saw" noise often repeatedly and well into the night.

Colour: Blue-grey neck area, brown-grey back and wings. White marks just near wings. Beak and Legs; yellow.

SPUR-WINGED PLOVER

A very common bird around the coast and also on farms. It will often swoop at people when defending a nest or young birds. It has a spur on the front joint of its wings.

Voice: Rapid "keeks" often, and at night as well as by day.

Colour: Mask and beak; yellow, Head and Collar; black. Wings; Light brown-grey, Neck and Underside; white, Legs; red.

GREY FANTAIL

A common bird in gardens, rainforest and open forest the Grey Fantail is inquisitive and unafraid. It is easy to recognise because of its zig-zagging flight and its tail which has earnt it the nickname of Cranky Fan. It eats insects.

Voice: Trilling and chattering.

Colour: Dark grey except for chest and face markings.

SWIFT PARROT

The Swift or Green Parrot is a regular visitor to farmyards and orchards. It breeds in Tasmania and migrates to the mainland during winter.

It feeds on nectar, berries, fruit and insects.

Voice:	A high-pitched, chattering, "clink-clink" noise.
Colour:	Mostly green with splashes of red, blue and yellow. Beak and claws are grey.

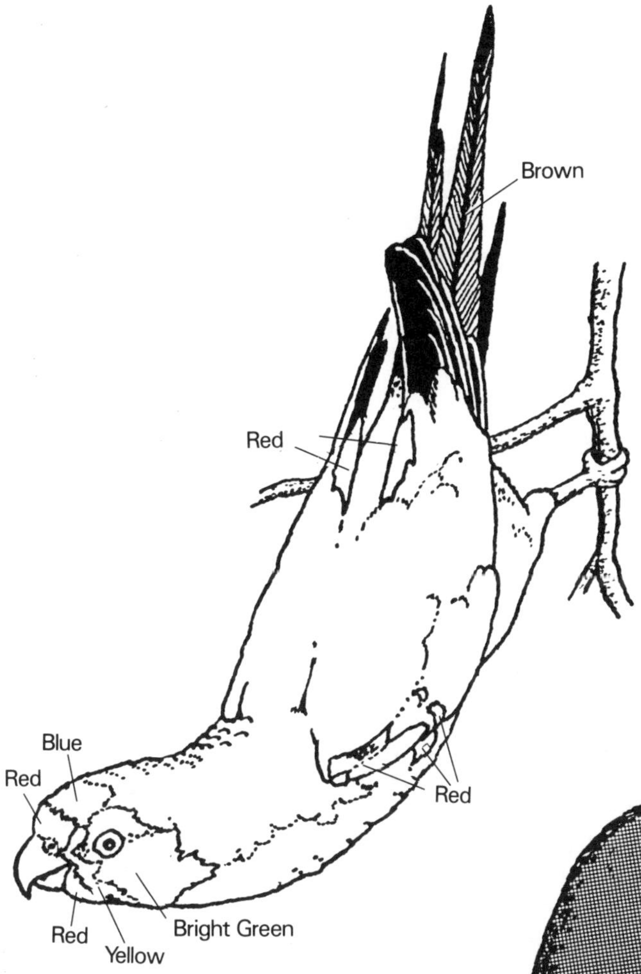

SUPERB BLUE WREN

This pretty little tame bird lives mostly in open forest and scrub but is also a common visitor to parks and gardens.

There are other types of Wren on the mainland but the Tasmanian variety is a species on its own and was first sighted and painted in 1777 by William Anderson, a surgeon on Captain Cook's last voyage.

Voice:	A light trilling like the tinkling of a small alarm clock.
Colour:	Male:- Head; black with bright blue markings, Chest; purple-blue, Wings; dark grey, Tail; black with blue tinge, Underneath; light grey. Female:- Head and wings; brown-grey, Underneath; light grey, Beak; brown.

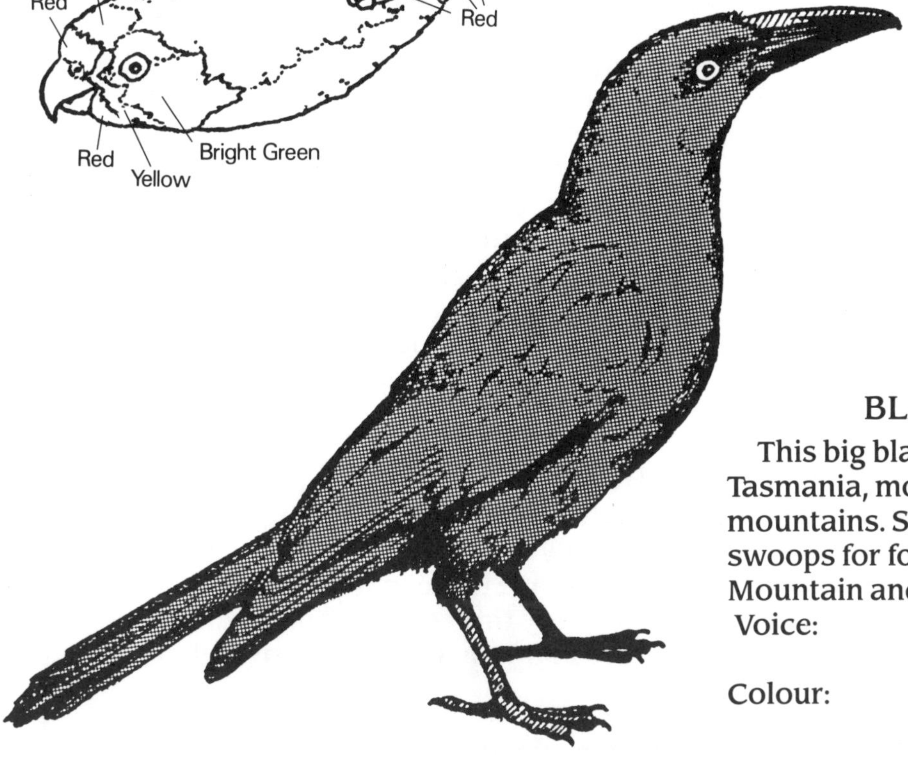

BLACK CURRAWONG

This big black bird is only found in Tasmania, most commonly in the mountains. Sometimes it is very tame and swoops for food, especially at Cradle Mountain and Lake St. Clair.

Voice:	Very lound "Kar-week-week-kar."
Colour:	Black all over with bright yellow eyes.

EASTERN SPINEBILL

This pretty bird is easily recognised by the fact that it feeds on the nectar of flowers and hovers like a hummingbird while feeding. It visits gardens but is shy and flies off swiftly if disturbed.

Voice: A series of rapid piping notes.

Colour: Top of head and wings; dull black with a blue tinge, Throat; black with white "Collar." Back and underside; chestnut brown.

SCARLET ROBIN

The Scarlet Robin is an eye-catching little bird common in open forest and farmland.

Colour: Black and white with a deep red chest patch.

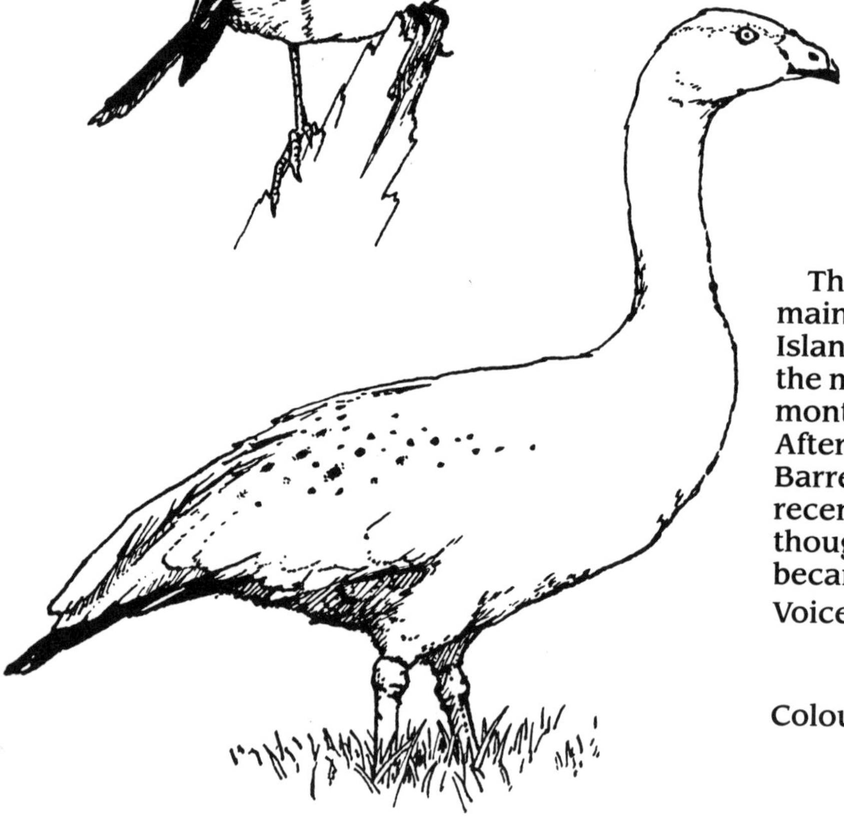

CAPE BARREN GOOSE

This large, unique bird lives and breeds mainly in the Bass Strait Islands and Maria Island. It does visit parts of Tasmania and the mainland, mainly during the summer months to forrage for grasses and seeds. After the sealing industry died out, the Cape Barren Goose was hunted for food and more recently farmers shot it because they thought it was a pest. As a result, it nearly became extinct. Today it is protected.

Voice: usually quiet, except for low grunts.
Noisy when flying.

Colour: body; grey, top of head; white, beak; bright greenish yellow, legs; pink with black feet.

LAUGHING KOOKABURRA

The Kookaburra is probably Australia's most famous bird and sure enough you will probably hear them "laughing" in Tasmania. But they are not native to Tasmania. In fact they were brought to Tasmania early this century. Their numbers are increasing and they are common in the eastern half of Tassie.

YELLOW TAILED BLACK COCKATOO

The Black Cockatoos are Australia's largest parrot. They move about over large areas usually preferring the mountains in summer and the coast or low hills in winter. Sometimes in the bush you will see a tree or a log that has been ripped open by Cockatoos' powerful beaks. They eat the larvae of wood boring grubs.

Voice: Loud screeches.
Colour: Dark brown all over with yellow patches on their cheeks and under the tail.

SWAMPHEN

The Swamphen is found all over Australia except in the driest desert areas. In Tasmania it is a very common sight and the Tasmanian birds are larger. It flies awkwardly and seems to prefer walking. As it walks or swims, it flicks it's tail.

Colour: Black head and wings with a deep purple-blue chest. Legs and beak; red.

BLACK SWAN

I was surprised to see swans in Tassie but they are here, and in large flocks. You can see them just near the bridge at Bridgewater, at Moulting Lagoon on the East Coast, along the Tamar River or at Lake Dulverton in Oatlands.

Colour: Black with white wing tips and tail tips. Nose and Eyes; red except for white patch on beak.

THE FOREST STORY

Even after nearly 200 years of logging almost half of Tasmania is still covered by forest. Gum trees (eucalyptus) are common here, as they are elsewhere in Australia, but there are many unusual plants that grow in Tasmania. Here is a rough guide to some of them. Plants marked with this symbol, E, are endemic, which means that they grow only in Tasmania and nowhere else.

There are 15 types of Eucalyptus or Gum Tree in Tasmania. The timber from 3 of them is known as Tasmanian Oak. As well being used for building, Tasmanian eucalypts are used for paper making and for woodchips which are sent to Japan.

The Tasmanian Blue Gum is now the most commonly grown eucalypt world-wide.

Blackwood, compact tree with blackish trunk.

The BLACKWOOD is a member of the Wattle family and grows throughout the State. It is often seen as a thick clumpy tree in paddocks in the North-West. Its rich coloured timber is prized by furniture makers.

PENCIL PINES grow extensively on the Central Plateau, especially around lakes and streams. It is very slow growing and some forests are over a thousand years old.

Sassafras, leaves; glossy green on top, dull white-green underneath.

Celery Top Pine, E, light green leaves.

The CELERY TOP PINE and SASSAFRAS are found only in rainforest and are both conical in shape. The timber of the Celery Top is very durable making it ideal for kitchens, windowframes and boat decks. The bark and leaves of the Sassafras give off a spicy cinnamon smell when crushed. The timber is used for panneling and furniture.

Pencil Pine, E

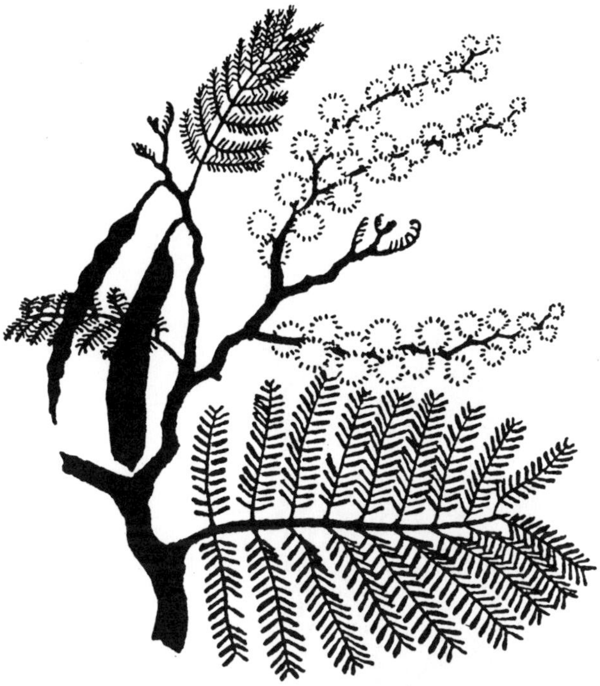

Silver Wattle, blossom yellow, seed pods purple.

Myrtle, young shoots can be yellow, orange or red.

The SILVER WATTLE is common thoughout most of Tasmania. In July and August they are covered in yellow blossom and are a stunning sight on fine winter days. The Silver Wattle is related to the pea family and can be seen through the summer covered in purple seed pods.

The FAGUS is Tasmania's only deciduous tree. It grows in a tangle on the wild slopes of the western mountains. Many people flock to Cradle Mountain in April to see the bright colours of its autumn leaves

The MYRTLE is the most common tree in Tasmania's rainforests growing to 50 metres. Myrtle forests are dark, mossy, mysterious places. The pink timber is used for furniture veneers and flooring.

HUON PINE is very famous as an excellent timber for boatbuilding. The timber is very oily which makes the timber impervious to insects and water. The tree only grows in the wettest parts of South-West Tasmania and grows so slowly that some trees are 2 300 YEARS OLD.

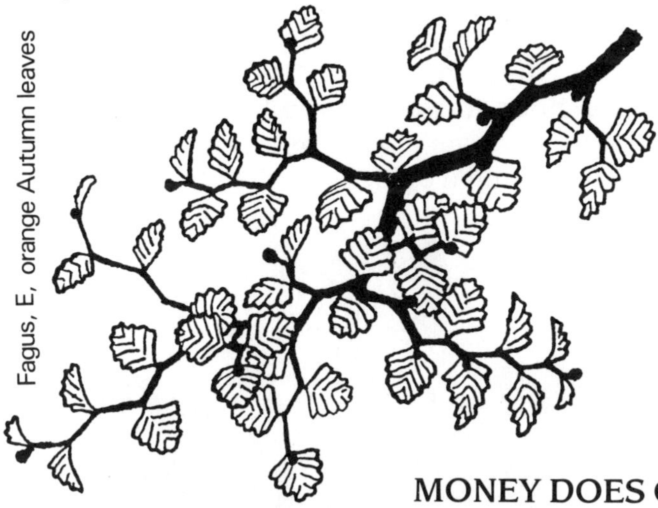

Fagus, E, orange Autumn leaves

Huon Pine, E, delicate drooping foliage.

MONEY DOES GROW ON TREES!

Tasmania has always been rich in natural resources. In the early days of settlement there were three resources which played a key role in Tasmania's development. They were seals, whales and trees.

Unfortunately, seals and whales were killed in such huge numbers that the industries based on them became extinct.

The forest industry still survives, though there are many people who worry that without proper care, Tasmania's forests might suffer the same fate as the whales and seals.

Back in the early days of settlement timber was cut mainly for building houses and boats. The work was done by convicts.

Today the forest industry employs about 20 thousand Tasmanians and is worth over $200 million dollars each year.

Manfern

The MANFERN is Tasmania's largest fern sometimes reaching a height of 10 metres. It grows under the canopy of forests or in wet gullies.

The LEATHERWOOD is common in the wetter, western half of the State. Its timber is used for furniture but its real claim to fame is the honey produced from the white flowers which cover the trees in December and January.

Leatherwood, E, delicate white flowers.

AS TALL AS A FOOTBALL FIELD?
At a height of 100 metres the Tasmanian Swamp Gum is the second tallest tree in the world and is the world's tallest flowering plant.

The PANDANI or GIANT GRASS TREE thrives in the wet forests of the south-west or in mountain forests where the rainfall is high.

Pandani, E

Button Grass, E

BUTTONGRASS covers much of the south-west and many mountain plateaux. It grows, in clump shaped mounds, in areas that were repeatedly burnt by the Tasmanian Aborigines. It also grows where the soil is poor and/or very wet. The name comes from the shape of its flowerheads.

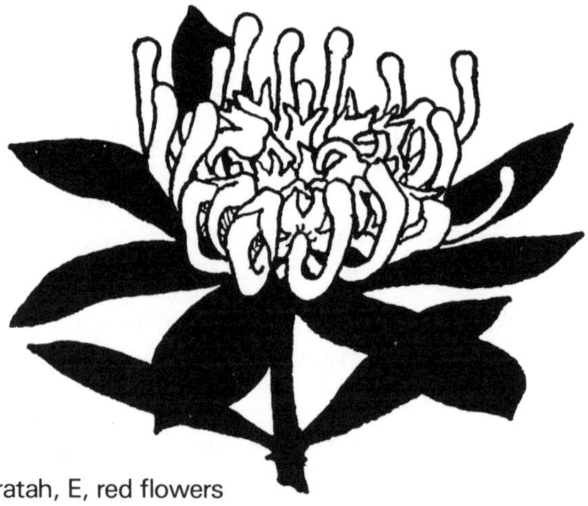

Waratah, E, red flowers

The Tasmanian WARATAH is different to the mainland Waratah. It grows to the height of a small tree and is covered in red flowers during November and December.

BUSHWALKING

Many people come to Tasmania, from all over the world, just to go bushwalking.

Walks in our wilderness areas can range from a twenty minute stroll to a week-long walk in rugged regions, without tracks, that have remained unchanged for thousands of years.

There are many do's and don'ts to follow when you go into these areas and I don't want to lecture you. Use your commonsense and treat the bush and animals with care and I'm sure you'll enjoy your walk.

However, for your own safety, have a look at the list of bushwalker's clothing. I take this gear with me whether it's winter or summer. Many of Tassie's best walks include mountainous areas, where it can snow suddenly, even in summer. Some walkers have died simply because they did not take the right clothes.

Always stay close to the people you are walking with and always tell someone where you are going for your walk and when you expect to be back. Many parks have a special log book where you can write down this information.

Happy Walking.

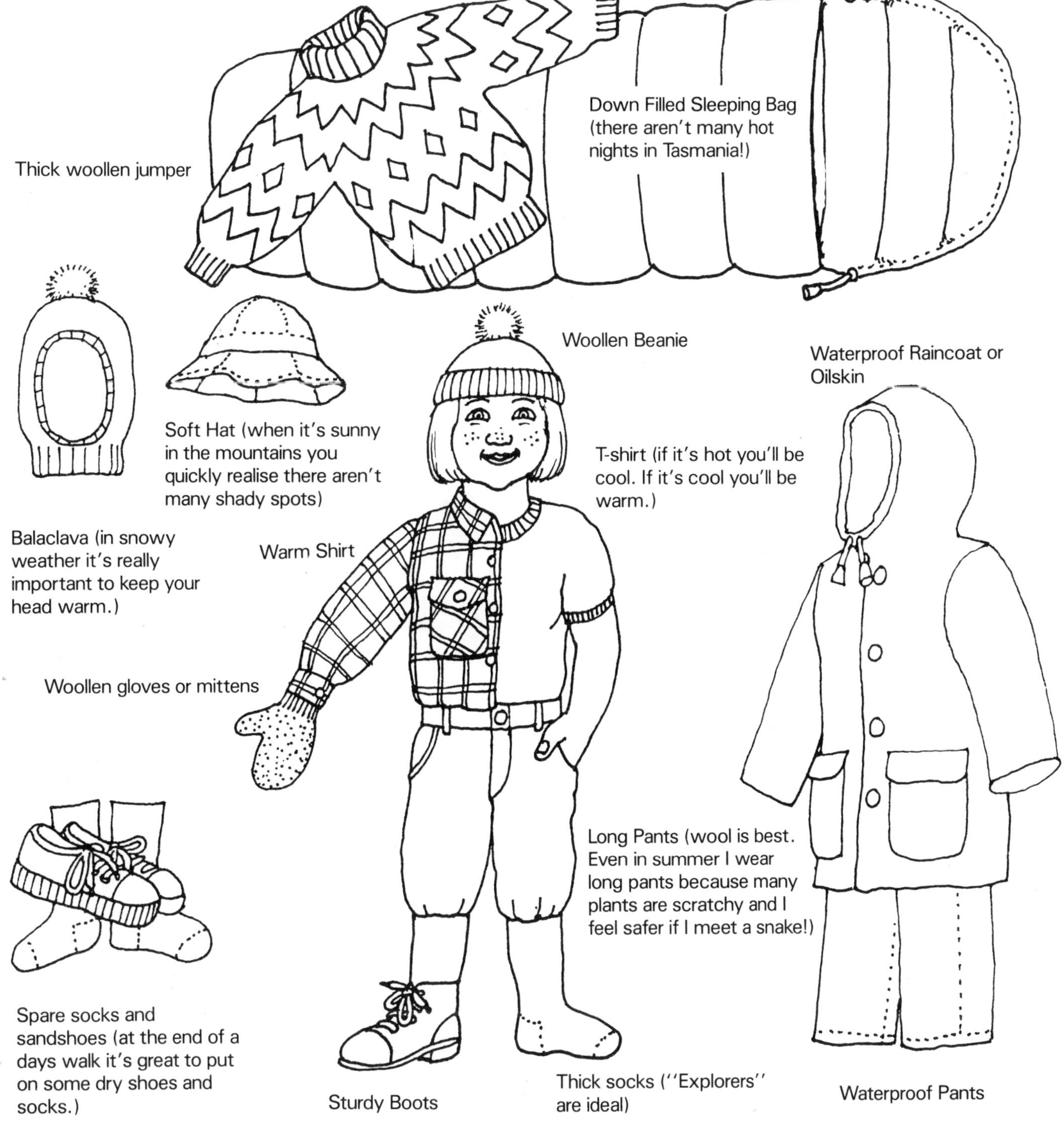

TASMANIAN TOUR GUIDE

Over the next few pages I have provided a list of attractions that I hope will interest you, the young traveller. Some of the suggestions have come from school children around the State.

There are many more places that you could visit. I can't fit them all in this book so I have picked the ones that I think you'll like best. You are the explorers, so I'll let you make some of your own discoveries.

Also, I can't show you detailed maps of all the streets and towns, so if you need more detailed information of places to see and where they are, visit a TASMANIAN TRAVEL CENTRE. They will be able to provide you with brochures. Also, they publish a complete guide to attractions, throughout Tasmania.

Don't forget to look in the NEWSPAPERS too, because there are many FUN EVENTS and FESTIVALS held throughout the year.

HOBART

Hobart is Australia's second oldest city. After Bass and Flinders had proven Tasmania was an island, it was feared that the French, who were exploring along the coast of Tasmania, might claim the island for France. (Back in those days France and England were often at war with each other.)

An order came from England, that new settlements be made on both sides of Bass Strait. One settlement, made just inside the mouth of Port Phillip Bay in Victoria failed, the other made in southern Tasmania became Hobart.

In September 1803, Lieutenant John Bowen, sailed up the Derwent River and landed at Risdon Cove where he set up camp. The population of forty-nine included soldiers, the better behaved convicts and three women.

A couple of months later, Lieutenant Collins arrived from the failed settlement in Victoria. After being joined by Collins, Bowen moved to Sullivan's Cove and named this settlement, Hobart Town.

Since those early times, Hobart has remained the centre of Government in Tasmania. Hobart has also been, a major port for the whaling industry, a centre for Antarctic expeditions and a popular tourist destination.

CADBURY'S CHOCOLATE FACTORY - **Bookings must be made to go on a tour of the Factory - Phone (03) 6249 0333 Admission charged.**

THINGS TO SEE AND DO IN HOBART

SALAMANCA PLACE - A row of warehouses built between 1835 and 1850. These were the boom years of whaling in Tasmania and in the park at the front of the buildings you can see the huge iron pots used to extract the valuable whale oil.

The buildings have been in continuous use since they were built. Today they house art and craft studios, theatre groups, galleries and shops.

Every Saturday at Salamanca is MARKET DAY. It is Tasmania's biggest market and well worth spending an hour or two there, either shopping, listening to the buskers or just being a "sticky-beak".

BATTERY POINT - Battery Point is a whole suburb of old homes and cottages built from the 1830's to the 1850's. It is located directly behind SALAMANCA PLACE and a walk through any of the region's streets is like stepping back in time.

There are two excellent MUSEUMS located in Battery Point. NARRYNA, built in 1836, houses a collection of colonial exhibits which show you what life was like in the 1800's. Admission is charged and it is open Tuesday to Friday all day, Saturday and Sunday 2-5pm only (closed Mondays) except during the month of July, when it is shut. NARRYNA is located at 103 Hampden Road.

SECHERON HOUSE at the end of Secheron Road is a MARITIME MUSEUM. It is open 7 days a week and admission for children is FREE.

PRINCES PARK is located right on the tip of Battery Point. It is a good place for adults to rest their feet while you have a play on the PLAY EQUIPMENT disguised as a SHIP.

CONSTITUTION DOCK and the PORT OF HOBART - The dock area is no longer the bustling port it was once, but it's still a great place to go for a walk. You can buy FISH and CHIPS from the FLOATING SHOPS in CONSTITUTION DOCK. You can see FISHING BOATS, YACHTS, the old MANLY FERRY, "NORTH HEAD", the TALL SHIP, "MAY QUEEN' or ships that go to the ANTARCTIC. There are also FERRIES which will take you to BELLERIVE or on RIVER TOURS. One ferry even travels to the CADBURY CHOCOLATE FACTORY.

THE TASMANIAN MUSEUM AND ART GALLERY is located just behind CONSTITUTION DOCK. The entrance is off Macquarie Street. Exhibits include TASMANIAN ANIMALS and WILDLIFE and PAINTINGS from the early days of Tasmania. The MUSEUM opens 7 days a week and admission is FREE except to some special exhibitions.

SWIMMING POOLS - Hobart Aquatic Centre, DOMAIN, olympic pool and wading pool, diving boards. Open all year round. Tasman Highway, near city roundabout. Admission charged.

GLENORCHY, olympic pool, waterslide. Open October to March. Anfield Street, Glenorchy. Admission charged.

CLARENCE, indoor heated pool. Open all year. Riawena Road, Montagu Bay. Admission charged.

These buildings at Salamanca Place, Hobart have been used continuously since the 1830's. Today they house artists, actors, craftsmen, shops and galleries. The gap between the two tall buildings, leads to Kelly's steps which will take you to historic Battery Point.

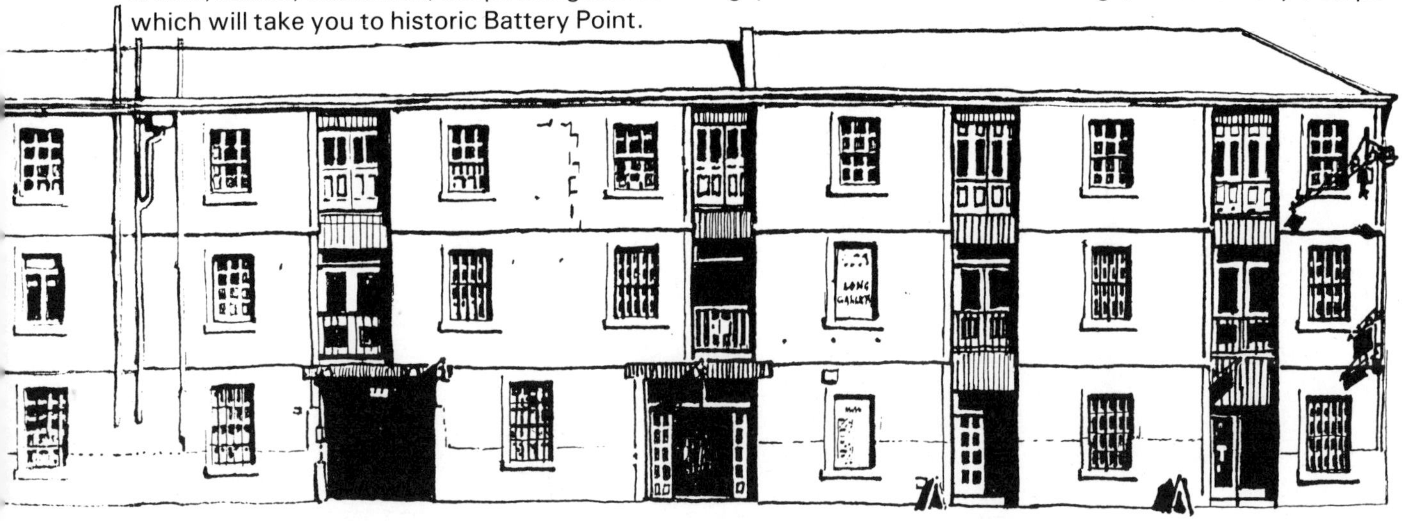

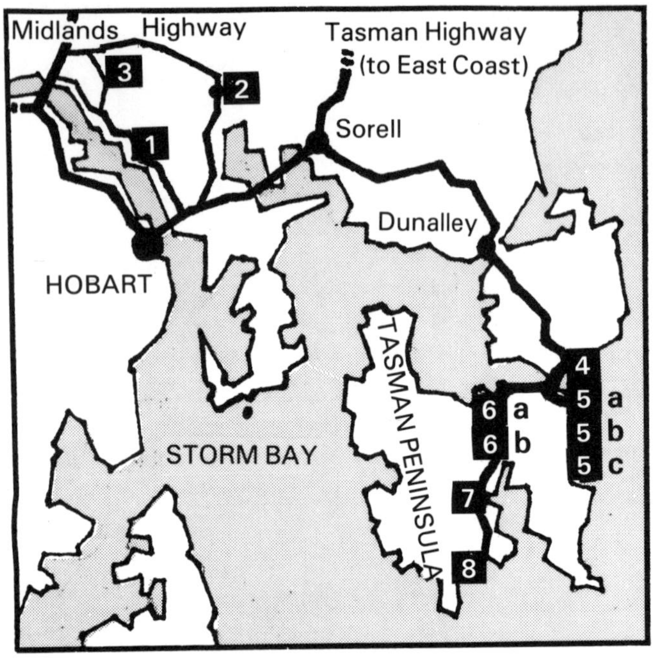

NORTH AND EAST OF HOBART

1 RISDON COVE HISTORIC SITE - Walks around the ruins of Tasmania's FIRST SETTLEMENT — FREE. Admission is charged for the display and film in the PYRAMIDS.

2 RICHMOND - An historic town with many fine CONVICT built buildings. RICHMOND BRIDGE is a great spot for picnics. Take some bread to feed the noisy DUCKS. RICHMOND GAOL shows the miserable conditions endured by the convicts. Tours 7 days a week. Admission charged.

3 BONORONG WILDLIFE PARK - Tasmanian Animals. Admission charged.

4 TESSELATED PAVEMENT - A unique formation that resembles a tiled floor. EAGLEHAWK NECK - The narrow strip of land that joins the Tasman Peninsula to Tasmania. It was here that a row of savage dogs were chained to stop convicts escaping.

5 a BLOWHOLE, **5** b TASMAN ARCH

5 c DEVILS KITCHEN - Unique rock formations. FREE. Nearby is DOOTOWN, a funny collection of cottages that all have the word DOO in their names!

6 a **THE BUSH MILL STEAM RAILWAY - Enjoy an exciting and scenic 4km return journey through the bush overlooking the water, with steep slopes, tight corners and a 70 metre long trestle bridge.**

6 b TASMANIAN DEVIL PARK - Tasmanian animals, video on TASMANIAN TIGER. Admission charged.

7 PORT ARTHUR HISTORIC SITE - Tasmania's most visited attraction. Tours of the PRISON, and other buildings daily, gives you an excellent glimpse into our convict past. Admission is charged.

8 **REMARKABLE CAVE - A rock formation, so named, because the mouth of the cave is shaped like a map of Tasmania. Count the steps. Be careful as the surf sometimes comes right through the cave. Views of the columned cliffs of CAPE RAOUL. FREE.**

BOXES

Here is a game for you to try. We normally play it in a square shape but just for fun here's a game in the shape of Tassie.

Aim: To make the most boxes.

Rules: Two players take turns joining the dots with lines one at a time, either like this, •—• or this, ⁞ Eventually they become boxes. □ So you can add up your scores, put an initial in each box you complete.

An Oast House near Bushy Park

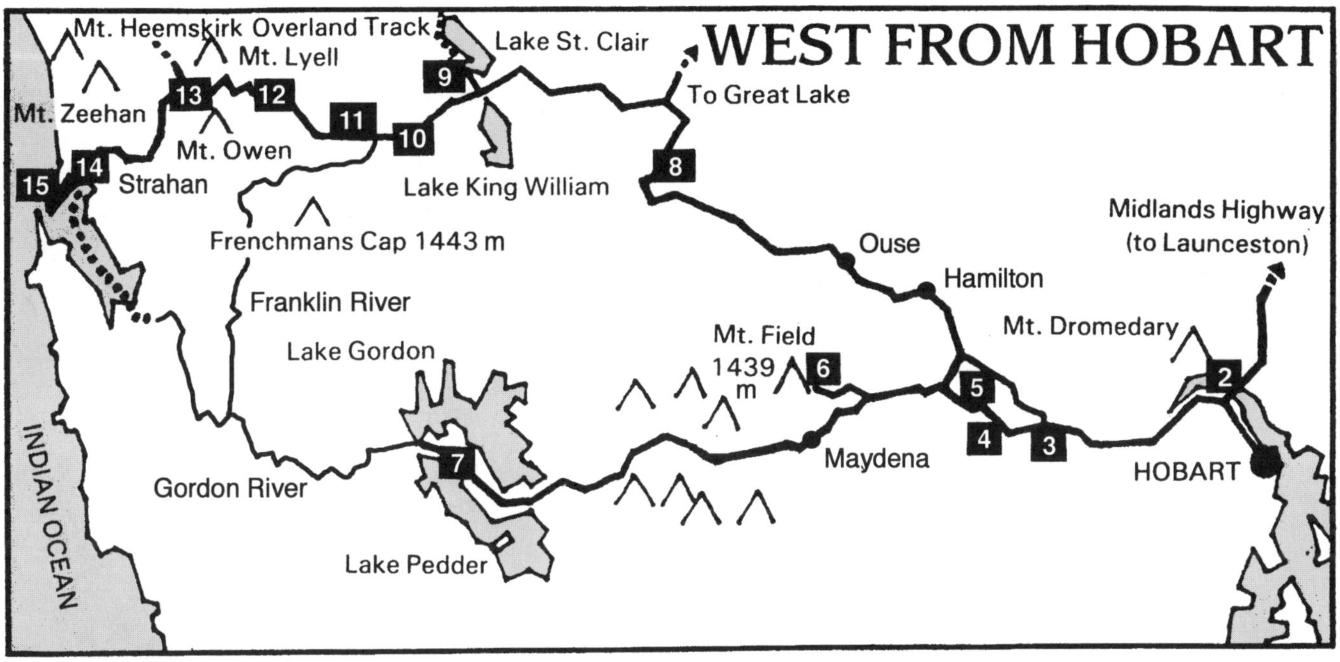

2 BLACK SWANS - Swans and Cygnets on the Derwent River.

3 NEW NORFOLK - Historic town, set on the wide banks of the Derwent River. JET BOAT RIDES. Fares charged. OAST HOUSE MUSEUM features a history of HOP growing. Admission charged. Swimming and walks beside river.

4 SALMON PONDS - Picnic spot and Tasmania's first TROUT HATCHERY. Feed the fish. Admission charged.

5 BUSHY PARK - An area dedicated to the growing of HOPS which are used in beer making. The plants grow up strings attached to a network of wires and poles. The harvested hops are dried in OAST HOUSES.

6 MOUNT FIELD NATIONAL PARK - Features: RUSSELL FALLS, a 10 minute walk from the park entrance. Spot the wallabies. Good BBQ sites. BUSHWALKS, MOUNTAIN SCENERY, WILDLIFE and SNOW SKIING in winter. 3 ROPE TOWS. EQUIPMENT HIRE. National Park Pass fee charged.

7 STRATHGORDON - A Hydro-Electric Commission village which was built during the construction of LAKE GORDON and the new LAKE PEDDER. SCENERY, TROUT FISHING, FERRY TRIPS. Guided Tours of the GORDON POWER STATION 7 days a week. Admission charged.

8 Look out for Hydro Power Stations around this area.

9 LAKE ST. CLAIR - This is the southern end of the CRADLE MOUNTAIN - LAKE ST. CLAIR NATIONAL PARK. The OVERLAND TRACK to Cradle Mountain begins here. Features:- Wallabies, Currawongs, Native Hens, Bushwalks. Admission to park charged.

10 KING WILLIAM SADDLE - Roadside stop featuring mountain views, including FRENCHMANS CAP. BUTTON GRASS.

11 NELSON FALLS - A ten minute easy walk through rainforest to pretty falls. Admission free.

12 GORMANSTOWN and LINDA - Old mining towns now deserted. Count the bends from here to Queenstown.

13 QUEENSTOWN - Tasmania's most famous mining town. It is surrounded by the bald peaks of Mt LYELL and MT OWEN. The bush that once surrounded Queenstown, fell victim to "ACID RAIN", created by the COPPER smelters and high rainfall. Ride the chairlift to the top of the hill. fares charged. Be sure to go on the ABT Wilderness Railway which travels through the bush. Various length trips are available and you can even pretend to be a gold prospector and go gold panning. Fares charged.

14 STRAHAN - A fishing port on MACQUARIE HARBOUR. There are daily FERRY trips, past the ruins of the dreaded convict settlement on SARAH ISLAND, to the GORDON RIVER where convicts once cut HUON PINES for boat building. Fares charged.

15 OCEAN BEACH and HELLS GATES - The dangerous entrance to Macquarie Harbour. It was near here that ABEL TASMAN first sighted Tasmania. The mountains at the northern end of the beach are named after his two ships, the ZEEHAN and the HEEMSKIRK.

TROUT FISHING

Adults need to buy a licence to fish for trout but if you are under 14 you can catch them for free!

Trout are not native to Tasmania. They were first introduced in 1864. Today, Rainbow and Brown trout can be spotted in just about every stream and lake throughout the State.

If you want to see and feed hundreds of trout at once then visit the Salmon Ponds. The ponds, just outside of New Norfolk, are where trout were first raised in Tasmania before they were released into the wild. It's a great spot for a picnic and as well as the museum the ponds are full of huge, greedy trout.

SPOT THE CHANGES There are 10 differences between these two pictures. Can you spot them all? The answers are on page 33.

ANSWERS TO CROSSWORD

ACROSS			DOWN		
3. snow	8. dam	16. apple	1. rapid	7. hut	15. oil
5. fur	10. pest	17. Launceston	2. Nut	9. ash	18. climb
6. paw	12. mine	20. skiing	3. swim	10. possums	19. tiger
7. Hobart	13. ba	21. bear	4. wine	11. sun	
	14. hops		5. Franklin	12. map	
				13. Bass	

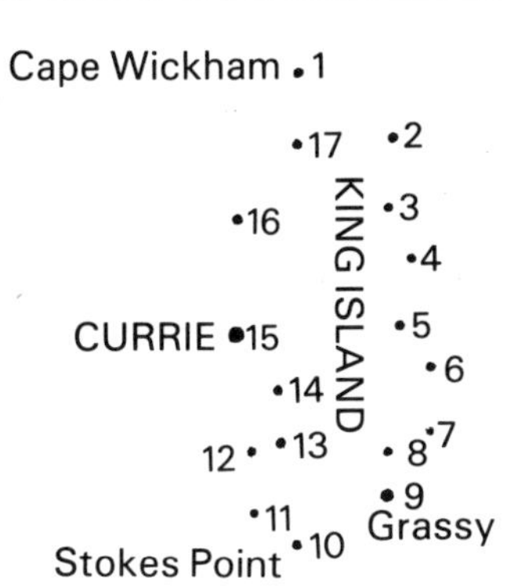

ATTENTION! Tasmanians get very angry if they are left off maps of Australia. Likewise, King and Flinders Islanders are furious if they get left off maps of Tasmania.

Most tourists don't get to the islands, so I have not shown them in the guide. HOWEVER both islands are very beautiful and WELL WORTH A VISIT.

Join the dots to reveal the Islands.

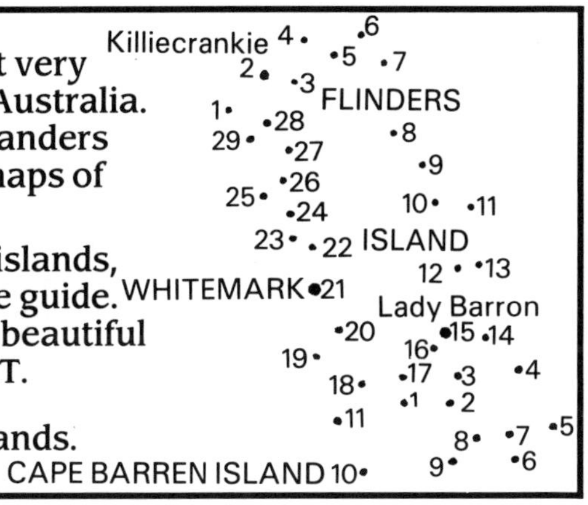

Tasmanian Tiger. Many people think that it still exists in rugged parts of the state.

TASMANIAN TIGER

Colour: Cream with dark brown stripes.

Size: 1.3 metres long.

Distribution: Extinct but some people believe it still exists in very rough thickly forested areas, especially the central and northern highlands and forests in the North-West and North-East.

Food: Wallabies and smaller animals.

Notes: It used to live in caves and rocky overhangs. It hunted at night in open country. Unfortunately when white settlers brought sheep to Tasmania the Tiger found them an easy source of food. The farmers responded by shooting them. The Government had a bounty of one pound for every dead Tiger. Between 1888 and 1912, 2184 were shot.

Fossils of Tasmanian Tigers and Devils have been found on the mainland but it is thought that they died out there because of the introduction of the Dingo to Australia.

The last Tasmanian Tiger died in captivity in 1936. Since then however, many people claim to have seen them and some wildlife experts believe they may still be here. All reported sightings are treated seriously, so keep a look out.

There is one Tasmanian animal that is definitely extinct, that is the Emu. It once lived in grassy areas around the coast. It was slightly smaller than the mainland Emu. The last one died in captivity in 1873.

Spot the Changes Answers

1. Title changed from fishing to skiing.
2. Splash above tree gone.
3. Spot on fish missing.
4. Cooking pot changed.
5. Rear tent pole changed.
6. Reflection of log missing.
7. Fisherman's ear changed.
8. Fisherman's fingers gone.
9. Dots on button missing.
10. Line of upper gumboot missing.

MIDLANDS AND LAKE HIGHWAYS

1 OATLANDS - HISTORIC TOWN. This is my favourite town in the Midlands. It is a great place for a walk, just to look at the many fine sandstone buildings and cottages. CALLINGTON MILL has been restored by the National Trust. LAKE DULVERTON features BLACK SWANS, picnic spots and is home to a MONSTER which some people claim to have seen from time to time.

2 SHAPED HEDGES - Mr. Jack Cashion, a D.M.R. worker began cutting these bushes during his lunch hour! There used to be nearly 100 but when the highway was re-routed many of them were bulldozed. See how many of them you can spot.

3 ROSS - Another HISTORIC TOWN. Picnic beside the famous ROSS BRIDGE and admire the carvings on it's three arches. Walk through the town or visit the TASMANIAN WOOL CENTRE to see a history of the region and a display on SUPERFINE WOOL growing. Admission to the Wool Centre is charged.

4a EVANDALE and **4b** CLARENDON - See Launceston Guide Page 36.

5 FRANKLIN HOUSE **6** ENTALLY HOUSE - See Launceston Guide Page 36.

7 BOTHWELL - HISTORIC TOWN. Another town with many old buildings. Australasian Golf Museum also in the town. Summer opening times 10a.m. till 4p.m. Winter opening times 11a.m. till 3p.m. Small admission fee.

8 GREAT LAKE - A man-made lake which is a popular destination for fishermen and hunters. TROUT FISHING, SNOWFALLS IN WINTER.

9 STUNNING VIEWS - From the edge of the WESTERN TIERS you can view the Midlands and Ben Lomond. MATTHEW BRADY had a lookout nearby.

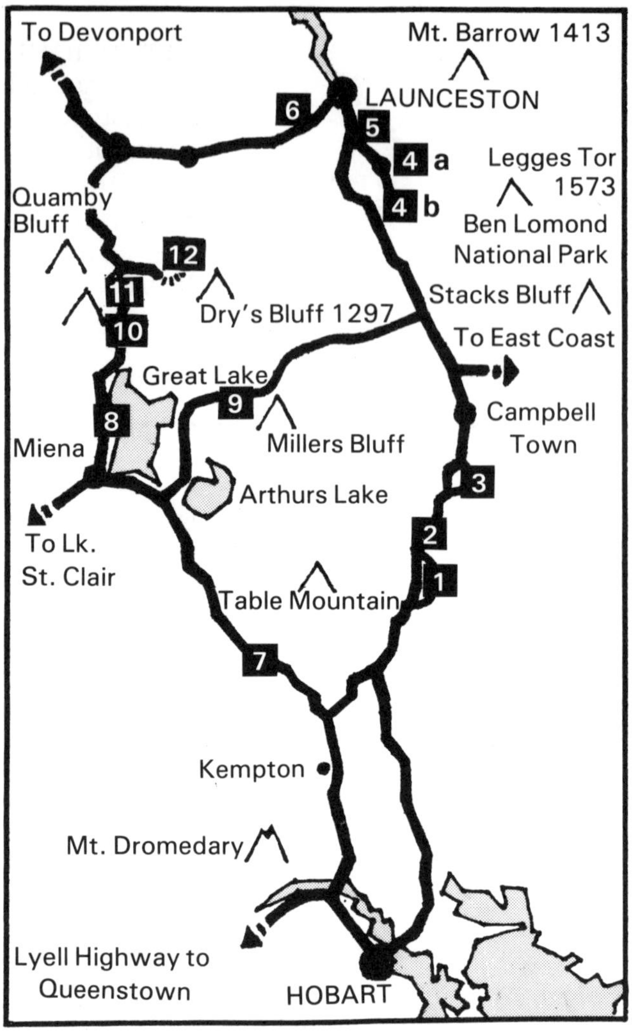

10 PINE LAKE - PROJECTION BLUFF AREA - PENCIL PINES, a native tree, grows by the lake which often freezes over in winter. Further along the road is a marked track to the summit of PROJECTION BLUFF. Views along the WESTERN TIERS and to QUAMBY BLUFF and BASS STRAIT! 2 hours return walk.

11 If you are travelling this road between May and August, keep a lookout for a shady overhang, it is often filled magically with ICICLES!

12 LIFFEY FALLS — Rainforest walks and pretty waterfalls. Picnic and Barbeque areas. 5 kilometres from Lake Highway. Admission free.

MONEY FROM THE SHEEP'S BACK. We all know sheep are grown for meat and wool but did you know that Tasmania's SUPERFINE WOOL fetches the WORLD'S HIGHEST PRICES?

Each year buyers come from all over the world to bid for our wool and each year Midlands properties vie with each other for the record price. In 1989 the highest price of 300,850 dollars went to "Connorville" near Cressy - for one bale!

To find out more about wool, visit the WAVERLEY WOOLLEN MILL in Launceston or the TASMANIAN WOOL CENTRE at Ross.

LAUNCESTON

Launceston is Tasmania's second largest city and is the third oldest city in Australia.

In 1804, Lieutenant-Colonel Paterson was sent to establish a settlement in northern Tasmania. The site he chose, just inside the mouth of the Tamar River, was called Yorktown.

In 1805, another settlement was made at the head of the Tamar Valley, where the North Esk and South Esk rivers meet. Farming in the Launceston district flourished and so 3½ years later Yorktown was abandoned in favour of Launceston.

Launceston grew slowly at first as a centre for mixed farming, timber and Bass Strait whaling. The goldrushes in Victoria brought new prosperity to the young town. Launceston was close to Melbourne. Food and timber were exported for high prices. This, and the discovery of gold at nearby Beaconsfield brought Launceston both people and prosperity. Many of Launceston's finest buildings were built during these boom years.

Tall ships used to come all the way, up river, to Launceston. Now George Town, nearer to Bass Strait, is the major port of the region.

Today, Launceston is still the major centre in northern Tasmania for both farming and industry.

In 1929 much of Launceston was flooded when heavy rains burst the old dam near Duck Reach Power Station. When you travel around Launceston, you will notice concrete walls and levees (mounds of earth) which were built to protect against further floods.

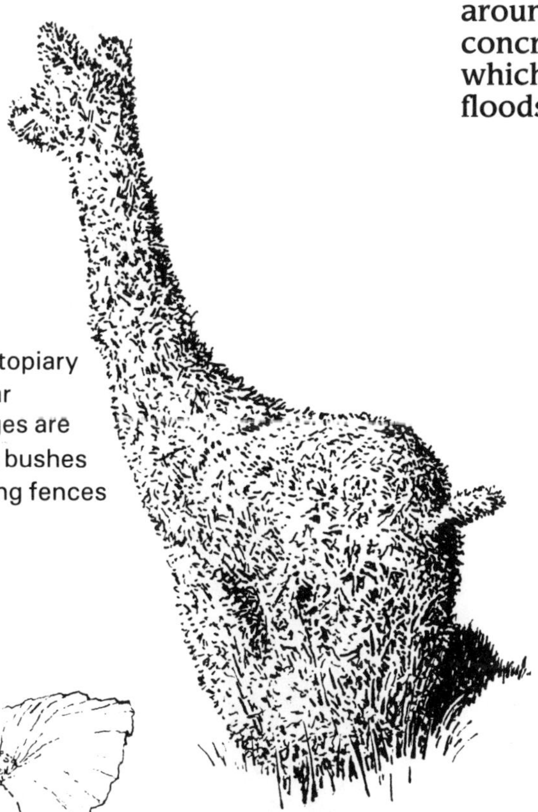

A shaped hedge or topiary beside the road near Oatlands. The hedges are cut from Hawthorn bushes which are used along fences throughout Tassie.

Callington Mill at Oatlands. One of the many old buildings in Tasmania's "Midlands".

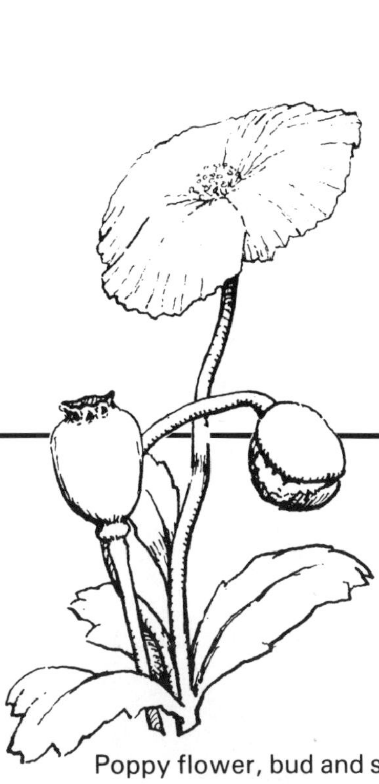

Poppy flower, bud and seed head.

PRETTY PINK PADDOCKS - Every Summer, usually in December, many paddocks around Tasmania turn pink with the blooms of OPIUM POPPIES.

The plants are allowed to dry out and then harvested. They are crushed and turned into a medicinal drug called Codiene Phosphate.

The black poppy seed is kept for use on breads and rolls. It contains no drugs.

DO NOT PICK POPPIES - IT IS AGAINST THE LAW

THINGS TO SEE AND DO IN LAUNCESTON

THE CATARACT GORGE AND CLIFF GROUNDS - A sheer valley cut through dolerite rock by the SOUTH ESK RIVER. Paths along the cliffs, link the city with the cliff grounds. Walkways are lit at night time. After heavy rains the gorge becomes a seething cauldron of RAPIDS and WHIRLPOOLS. Features: FORMAL GARDENS, CHAIRLIFT across gorge, PEACOCKS wandering about. Walk up to DUCK REACH from the SWINGING SUSPENSION BRIDGE to see Australia's first power station built in 1895.

CITY PARK - A large park near the city centre. Features: MONKEYS, DUCK POND, PLAY EQUIPMENT, OUTDOOR CHESS and gardens.

ROYAL PARK - A great spot for a walk by the Tamar, What looks like a big grandstand is actually a wall built to deflect future floods.

HOME POINT - Tamar River Cruises offers rides up the beautiful Tamar river. Fares charged.

QUEEN VICTORIA MUSEUM AND ART GALLERY - features: TASMANIAN ANIMALS, MINERALS, CONVICT ARTIFACTS, COLONIAL PAINTINGS and TRAVELLING EXHIBITIONS - Wellington Street opposite Cameron Street. Open daily. Also at Inveresk Railyards. Admission charged.

MARITIME MUSEUM - Features displays of Tassie's seafaring past including SEALING and WHALING. Corner of St John and Cimitiere Streets. Open daily. Sunday 2-4pm. Admission charged.

NATIONAL AUTOMOBILE MUSEUM OF TASMANIA - The museum prides itself in having possibly the best presentation in Australia. CARS and MOTORCYCLES spanning some 80 years and visitors can enjoy hearing some of the interesting histories surrounding the vehicles as they wander through time. Cimitiere Street, (opposite City Park). Admission charged.

SWIMMING POOLS - The GORGE , olympic sized pool and wading pool set in spectacular surroundings. Pool open between mid-October and March. Basin Road. FREE.

WINDMILL HILL, olympic and wading pools and waterslide. Open between October and March. Corner of York and High Streets. Admission charged.

RIVERSIDE, half olympic pool and waterslide. Open October to March. Eden Street, Riverside. Admission charged.

KIDS PARADISE - A great place to visit. 23 Racecourse Crescent. Admission charged.

FRANKLIN HOUSE, ENTALLY HOUSE - Historic homes all with excellent displays of colonial life. FRANKLIN HOUSE, Hobart Road, Youngtown. ENTALLY HOUSE, just off the Bass Highway, Hadspen. All buildings and grounds are open daily. Admission charged.

PENNY ROYAL - Visit the GUNPOWDER MILL and CORNMILL, ride the TRAM and climb the WINDMILL. Admission charged.

BEN LOMOND NATIONAL PARK - Legges Tor, 1573 metres above sea level, is Tassie's second highest peak. Jacob's Ladder, a zig-zag road between sheer cliffs is probably Australia's steepest road. Features: SCENIC VIEWS, MOUNTAIN SCENERY, BUSHWALKS , SKIING in winter. EIGHT SKI TOWS, TOBOGGANS and SKI EQUIPMENT for hire. National Park fee charged.

EVANDALE - Historic town near Launceston Airport featuring old buildings and a village atmosphere. EVANDALE MARKET on Sundays. CLARENDON historic home nearby.

Matthew Brady. Find out about him on the opposite page.

THE TAMAR VALLEY

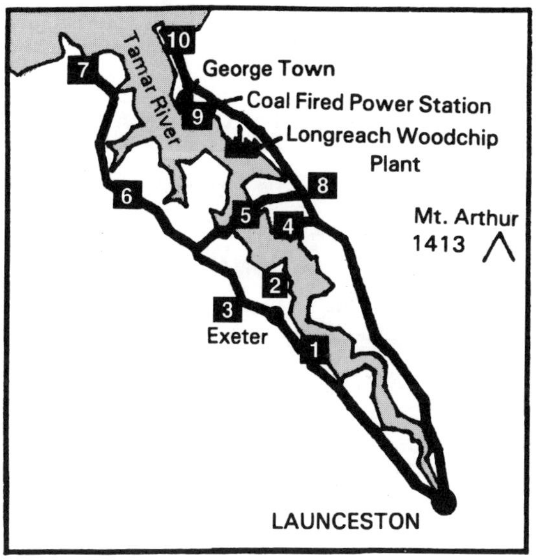

1 BRADY'S LOOKOUT - MATTHEW BRADY, the notorious bushranger, used this lookout, to swoop on unsuspecting travellers using the road below. Fantastic views of the Tamar Valley and eastern mountains.

2 KRAZY PUTT MINI GOLF - Great for all the family, 363 Gravelly Beach Road, Gravelly Beach. Admission charged.

3 GLENGARRY BUSH MAZE - 48 Jay Dee Road, Glengarry. Admission charged.

4 HILLWOOD - A berry farm where you pick your own STRAWBERRIES during summer. Train to play on.

5 BATMAN BRIDGE - An unusual looking bridge, named after John Batman, the founder of Melbourne. Because no strong foundation could be built on the eastern shore, the weight of the bridge is supported by the tower on the western bank. Look for whirlpools in this part of the river. Picnic areas.

6 BEACONSFIELD - Once the site of Tasmania's biggest GOLD MINE. You can walk around the large ruins of the old mine buildings and visit the museum. Admission charged.

7 GREENS BEACH - A popular holiday spot for Tasmanians. Safe swimming beaches.

8 LONGREACH WOODCHIP PLANT - Watch huge logs being turned into woodchips. FREE.

9 BELL BAY - An industrial area and port. Comalco make ALUMINIUM here because Tasmania provides plenty of electricity which is needed to make it.

10 LOW HEAD - A picturesque village with many fine old buildings and safe, swimming beaches. THE LOW HEAD PILOT STATION has an excellent MARITIME MUSEUM which opens daily. An admission fee is charged.

BUSHRANGERS

Life as a convict was usually awful. They worked long and hard, were flogged for misbehaviour and small crimes, were fed poorly and slept in cramped, dirty conditions.

Sometimes escape was possible but how could an escaped convict survive without food in the bush? There was only one way and that was to become a Bushranger. Many convicts, perhaps a couple of hundred did become bushrangers. Even an aborigine, named Musquito, who was brought to Tasmania became one.

They lived by raiding farmhouses and stealing horses, guns, money, food and clothing. Unfortunately, hanging was the punishment for bushranging and most of them ended their short careers on the end of a hangman's rope.

The most famous bushranger was Matthew Brady, the "Gentlemen's Bushranger." He was handsome and educated. He was transported to Sydney for forgery. From there he was sent to the dreaded prison at Macquarie Habour. With nine other convicts he escaped in a stolen boat. For nine days they rowed around the coast and landed not far from Hobart. From then on they lived as Bushrangers.

In one daring raid Brady and his gang ordered the servants to prepare a meal then sat down and dined with the family as if they were invited guests. Afterwards they thanked them for their hospitality and rode away with the loot.

With every raid the government grew angrier and finally decided to release a convict named Cowan to spy on Brady and his bunch. He became friendly with the gang and eventually told police where Brady was hiding. There was a huge shootout and nearly the whole gang was captured or killed. Brady escaped but he was badly wounded and could not travel for long.

He was washing his wounded leg in the Nile River when John Batman rode by. Brady surrended because he thought Batman would treat him fairly.

After two years of bushranging Brady was hung in Hobart.

LAUNCESTON TO MOLE CREEK AND DEVONPORT

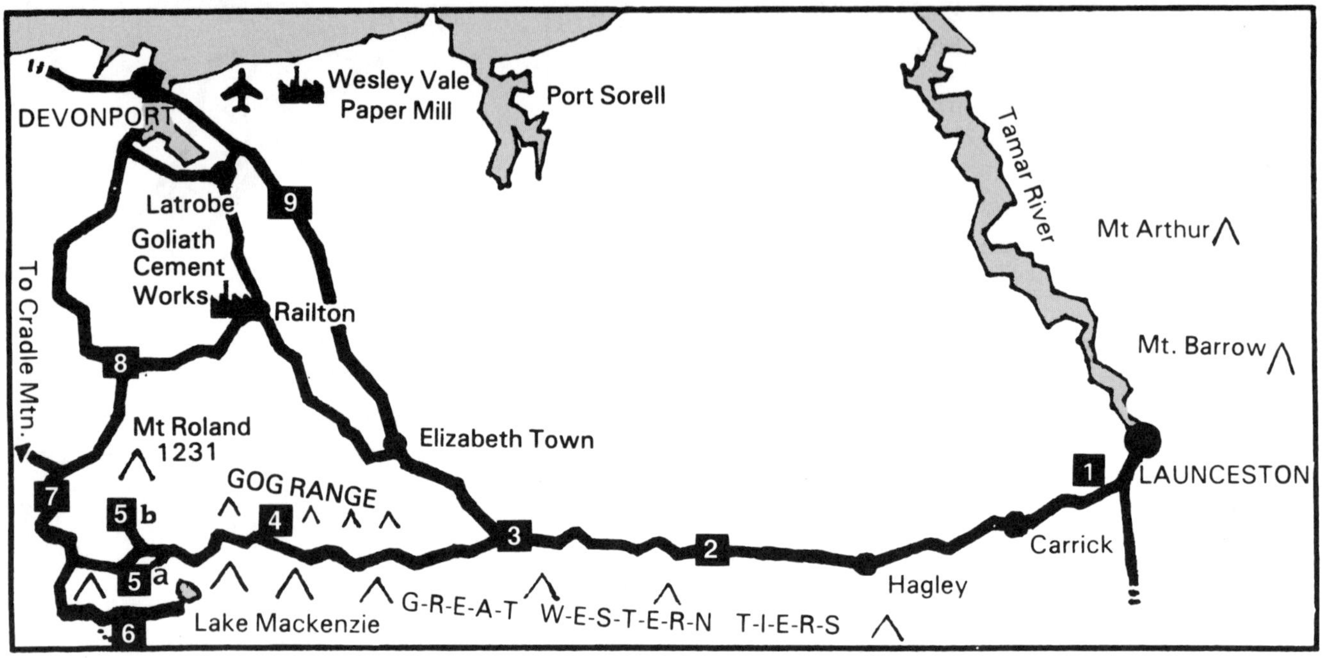

As the highway now bypasses some of these towns you may need to do a short detour to see some of the things listed.

1 ENTALLY HOUSE - See Launceston Guide Section.

2 WESTBURY - A large rural town with many historic buildings and a village green. Features: PEARNS STEAM WORLD. Before the invention of tractors huge steam engines were used instead of men and horses.

WESTBURY MAZE - Bass Highway, Westbury. Find the middle in a maze of hedges. Both these attractions are on the Bass Highway, Westbury. Admissions charged.

3 DELORAINE - Picture book town on Meander River with Quamby Bluff and the Great Western Tiers to the south. Just near the bridge is a PARK with an old train, play equipment and a weir. It is a good spot to stretch your legs.

4 TROWUNNA WILDLIFE PARK MOLE CREEK - An excellent place to see TASMANIAN ANIMALS and KOALAS, which are not native to Tasmania. Open 7days a week. Admission charged.

5a MARAKOOPA CAVE and **5b** KING SOLOMON CAVE - Limestone Caves set in rainforest surroundings. Picnic sites. Admission charged.

6 DEVIL'S GULLET - A breathtaking LOOKOUT set on top of huge cliffs. Views to Mt. Ossa and Cradle Mountain. 10 minute walk from car park on Lake Mackenzie road.

7 MT CLAUDE - High point on road with stunning views.

8 SHEFFIELD - A farming town set in picture book countryside. Many local buildings have MURALS painted on them. Views to Mt. ROLAND. Nearby is LAKE BARRINGTON a man-made lake used for ROWING competitions and WATER-SKIING.

9 RICH RED SOIL - The deep volcanic soils around Sassafras are some of the richest soils in Australia. Potatoes, Peas, Onions, Carrots, Brussell Sprouts, Cauliflowers and many other vegetables are grown for EXPORT.

BATMAN: Did you know, that as well as capturing Matthew Brady, John Batman was the founder of Australia's second largest city, Melbourne

The sport of woodchopping originated in Tassie during the 1870's. Tasmania has produced many World Champions.

Colour in this scene from Marakoopa Cave with yellow, orange and brown.

"GUGGENHIEM"

This is a game I first played in Tasmania. We call it Guggenhiem — I don't know why. It can be played by people of all ages and is best with only two or three players.

SAMPLE GAME

T	R	U	N	K	5
O	W	N	E	M	1
T	A	D	D	I	1
E	R	E	A	L	3
M	O	R	A	L	5
5	1	5	0	3	

Aim: To make as many words as possible. Highest score wins.

Rules: Each player draws up a grid of 6 lines down by 6 lines across. That will leave you with a large square made up of 25 small squares. Taking it in turns each player calls any letter of the alphabet. You must write down each letter called. When all the squares are full add up your scores.

Scoring: Words of 5 letters are worth 5 points. Words of 4 letters are worth 3 points and words of 3 letters are worth 1 point. 2 letter words do not score. Only score words up and down not diagonally.

THE NORTH WEST and WEST COASTS

1 DEVONPORT BLUFF - The Bluff at Devonport is an interesting area to visit. Features include:— ABORIGINAL ROCK CARVINGS, follow the footprints from just near the LIGHTHOUSE, TIAGARRA ABORIGINAL CENTRE, by the lighthouse is open daily. Admission is charged. SWIMMING BEACH. Nearby is a SKATEBOARD BOWL, PLAYGROUND and BIKE HIRE Centre. Just along Victoria Parade is the Devonport BREAKWATER. Many ships were wrecked near here, the dredge "G Ward Cole" is still aground on the rocks. MARITIME MUSEUM which is open Tuesday to Sunday is also along Victoria Parade. Admission charged.

2 DON RIVER RAILWAY - All aboard here, for a steam powered ride, on Tasmania's ONLY PASSENGER TRAIN! A fare is charged.

3 CRADLE MOUNTAIN - The OVERLAND TRACK to LAKE ST. CLAIR begins here but there are also many short walks and even a strenuous day walk to the SUMMIT, which is well worth the effort, if the weather's fine. Other features:— DOVE LAKE, WALDHEIM, the home of pioneer GUSTAVE WEINDORFER, tame WALLABIES and PADEMELONS,

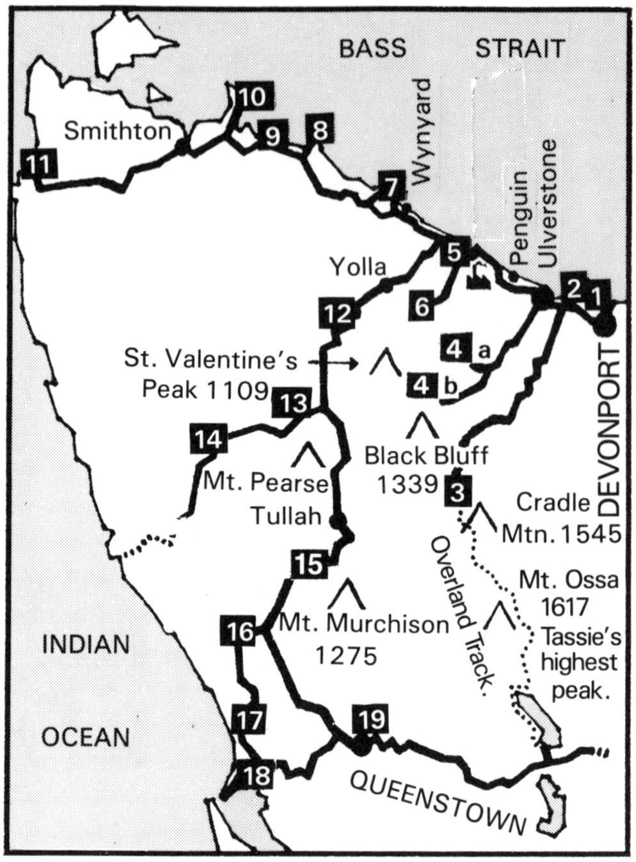

FAGUS and SNOW in winter and spring. National Park fee applies

4 a GUNNS PLAINS CAVES — Limestone Caves open daily. Admission charged.
4 b LEVEN CANYON is a spectacular valley cut by the LEVEN RIVER which runs beneath the towering BLACK BLUFF. Walks and Picnic spots.

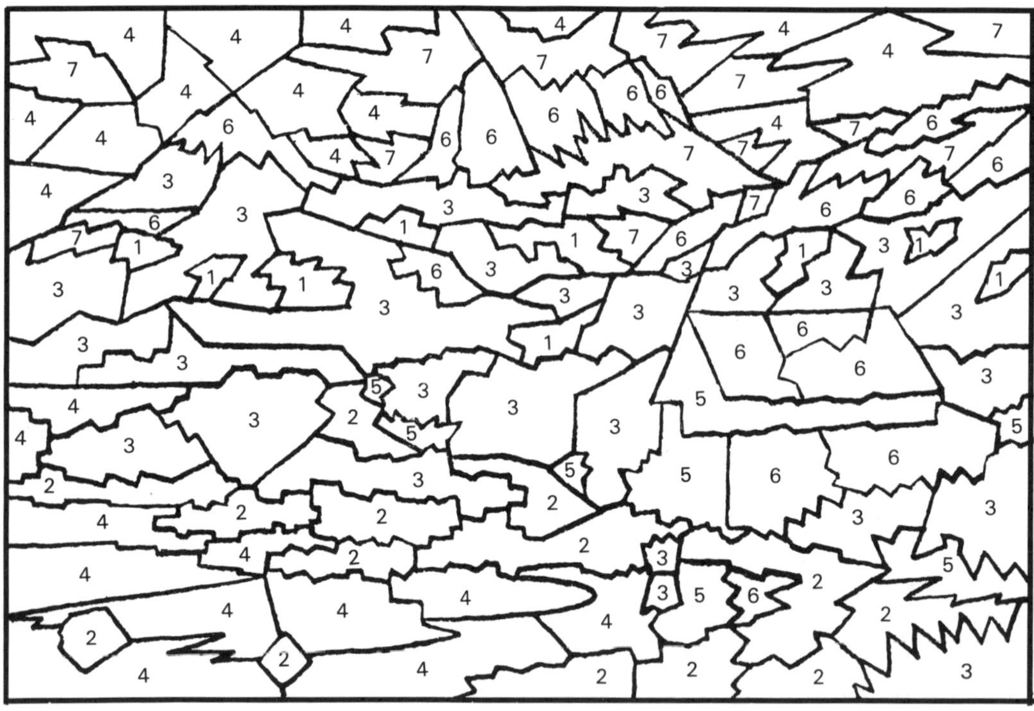

COLOUR BY NUMBER

1. Orange
2. Light Brown or Yellow
3. Green
4. Blue
5. Black
6. Grey or Brown
7. Leave white

This is a picture of . . . .
. . . .

5 BURNIE - A large industrial town which is also an export centre for the West Coast including the AUSTRALIAN PAPER FACTORY which produces quality paper. Play equipment and waterfall at Burnie Memorial Park.

6 GUIDE FALLS - There are many waterfalls in the picturesque Ridgley area but Guide Falls is the easiest to visit. Look out for the unusual BASALT rocks and ST VALENTINES PEAK in the distance. Picnic spots.

7 TABLE CAPE and FOSSIL BLUFF - Table Cape towers above the rich farming country nearby. There is a LIGHTHOUSE on the cape and nearby there is a LOOKOUT with spectacular views. Just below the cape is a good SWIMMING BEACH and nearby there are FOSSILS on the headland. Drive along the scenic route to BOAT HARBOUR to see the ocean.

8 ROCKY CAPE NATIONAL PARK - Matthew Flinders named this cape surrounded by clear blue water. SWIMMING, VIEWS, BUSHWALKS, ABORIGINAL CAVES and WILDFLOWERS. Admission charged.

9 PORT LATTA - This gigantic factory in the "middle of nowhere" is at the end of a pipeline that runs from SAVAGE RIVER. Iron ore is exported to Japan from here. Nearby is a little playground with good views of the NUT and picnic spots. It is called BRICKMAKERS BEACH.

10 STANLEY - This is my FAVOURITE TOWN! I always feel sorry for visitors who miss it. STANLEY is an HISTORIC TOWN and so it features many old buildings including HIGHFIELD, the headquarters of the old Van Diemen's Land Company. You can climb the NUT or ride on the chairlift to the top to see the MUTTONBIRD burrows and the fantastic VIEWS or walk around the GRAVEYARD below. FISH off the wharves or walk along the beaches.

11 MARRAWAH - This is as far WEST as you can go in Tassie. Greens Beach is popular with local surfers and is a great place for BEACHCOMBING. MT CAMERON WEST at the end of the beach is a spectacular place to sit and watch the swells coming in from the INDIAN OCEAN.

12 HELLYER GORGE - Henry Hellyer explored this region in the 1830's - can you imagine exploring the unknown in these dark forests? Picnic spots and nice forest walks.

13 WARATAH - Once the world's richest TIN MINE. Today it is a sleepy town with the wonderful ruins of MT BISCHOFF which you can visit for FREE. BE CAREFUL THERE ARE SOME DEEP HOLES. Keep a lookout for OLD ORE TRUCKS and PYRITE CRYSTALS which are also called FOOL'S GOLD.

14 SAVAGE RIVER - Iron was discovered years before the mine opened, but Savage River was so remote, that there was no way for the iron-ore to be taken to a port. Today it travels as a slurry, through a pipeline, all the way to PORT LATTA. 9

The PIEMAN RIVER gets its unusual name from an escaped convict, ALEXANDER PEARCE. He was caught on the river bank carrying the remains of a fellow escapee he had KILLED FOR FOOD. Pearce had been imprisoned for selling tainted (bad) pies.

15 ROSEBERY - A ZINC mining town.

16 ZEEHAN - The town is named after one of TASMAN'S SHIPS. Zeehan was once a bustling SILVER and LEAD mining town. In the 1880's it had 26 Hotels and a population of 10,000! It is much quieter today but you can still see some of the fine buildings from its boom times. THE WEST COAST PIONEER'S MUSEUM has one of the best collections of MINERALS as well as many interesting displays. It is open daily. Admission fee charged.

17 A NEW ROAD - This road follows an old railway track that linked ZEEHAN and STRAHAN. The HENTY DUNES are a magnificent sight. The ROARING FORTIES are blowing the sand inland, a metre each year. Picnic sites are nearby.

18 STRAHAN - See Hobart to Queenstown Guide Section.

19 QUEENSTOWN - See Hobart to Queenstown Guide Section.

THE EAST COAST

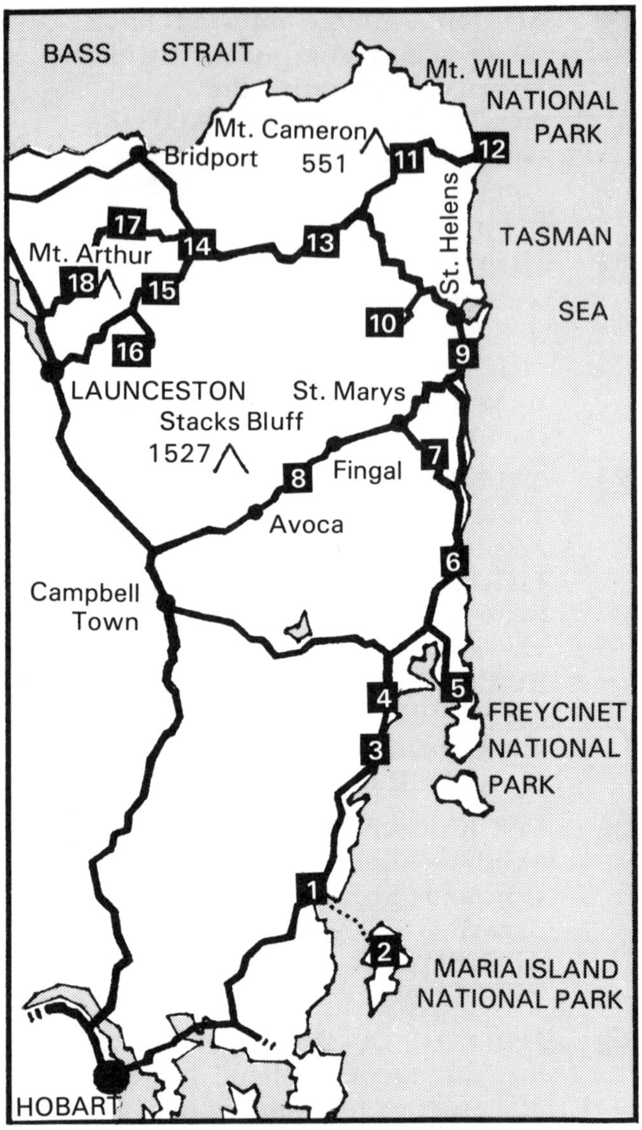

1 ORFORD and TRIABUNNA - Many of Tasmania's old buildings were built from SANDSTONE quarried at Orford. Triabunna has a huge WOODCHIP PLANT which exports woodchips to Japan. The one hour FERRY trip to MARIA ISLAND leaves from the nearby EASTCOASTER RESORT.

2 MARIA ISLAND - Abel TASMAN named the island after the wife of Anthony Van Diemen. A resident tribe of Aborigines used to live on the island which is now a NATIONAL PARK. Features: EMUS, CAPE BARREN GEESE, FORESTER KANGAROOS, CONVICT RUINS, Camping, Fishing, Bushwalks and Rock climbing. Admission charged.

3 SPIKY BRIDGE - This curious bridge, built in 1843, was still in use until just a few years ago. Do you have any idea why it has the SPIKES? Nobody else seems to know why. There are sheltered beaches nearby which feature MIDDENS, VIEWS OF THE FREYCINET PENINSULA.

4 SWANSEA - Named after SWANS in nearby MOULTING LAGOON. SWANSEA BARK MILL demonstrates how ANIMAL SKINS are tanned. Open daily and admission is charged.

5 COLES BAY -A small holiday village on the edge of the FREYCINET NATIONAL PARK. RED GRANITE quarried from THE HAZARDS can be seen on buildings throughout Australia. Features: STUNNING COASTAL SCENERY, BUSHWALKS, FISHING, CAMPING and SWIMMING. National Park fee charged.

6 BICHENO - A fishing and holiday town. Features: THE GULCH, which is a unique harbour, the BLOWHOLE, just south of the town, THE SEA LIFE CENTRE which has live SHARKS, CRAYFISH, SEA HORSES and more, and the EAST COAST NATURE WORLD where you can see birds and animals. Both the Sea Life and Bird Life Centres are open daily. Admission charged. Climb the hill to see views of the town and out to sea.

7 ELEPHANT PASS - Views of the coastline. Can you see an ELEPHANT lying down in the shape of the hills?

8 FINGAL VALLEY - A beautiful valley, overshadowed by Sphinx and Stacks Bluffs, which are at the southern end of BEN LOMOND NATIONAL PARK. Coal is mined at MT NICHOLAS and FINGAL.

9 BEACHES, BEACHES, BEACHES - This section of coast, from Falmouth to ST HELENS and right up to the northern tip is nearly all beach. The area is popular with Tasmanian holiday makers. SWIMMING, SAILING, FISHING.

10 ST COLUMBA FALLS An awe inspiring waterfall that thunders into the RAINFOREST below.

11 GLADSTONE - This region once supported dozens of TIN MINES, today only sleepy Gladstone survives. The GRANITE peaks of MT CAMERON tower over the flat countryside. Many people go GEMSTONE FOSSICKING in the nearby rivers.

12 EDDYSTONE LIGHTHOUSE - This superbly built granite tower is at the southern end of the MT WILLIAM NATIONAL PARK which was set aside as a reserve for the once common FORESTER KANGAROO. Beautiful swimming, beaches with UNUSUAL ROCK FORMATIONS. National Park fee charged.

13 DERBY and BRANXHOLM - Both towns are old mining centres. Today they service the farming and forestry industries. HOPS are now grown near Branxholm.

14 SCOTTSDALE - Centre of very rich, farmlands and lush forests. Scottsdale is the north-east's biggest town. The GENERAL JONES FACTORY freezes and packages a large variety of VEGETABLES FOR EXPORT.

15 THE SIDLING - Views of the rich Scottsdale district. Scenic lookout showing lovely farming country.

16 MT BARROW - A road takes you to just below the SUMMIT. There are walks, shelters, SNOW in winter and VIEWS IN ALL DIRECTIONS.

17 BRIDESTOWE LAVENDER FARM - This famous tourist attraction is open November to April, 9am - 5pm, 7 days (closed Christmas Day). May, September and October 10am - 4pm, Monday to Friday. June, July and August closed. The sight and smell of the PURPLE PADDOCKS is really memorable. Picnic areas. Admission charged.

18 LILYDALE DISTRICT - This pretty farming area nestled beneath MT ARTHUR is a popular picnic spot for the people of Launceston. HOLLYBANK is a dark forest of European trees with TOADSTOOLS growing beneath. Barbecues and walks. Admission charged. The W.A.G. WALKER RHODODENDRON RESERVE is only open from September 1st to December 15th and again from April 1st to May 31st. See it in spring when the Rhododendron trees are covered in BRIGHT FLOWERS. FREE.

Australian Fur Seal.
It's numbers are increasing again on rocks and islands along the East Coast. It is now a PROTECTED ANIMAL.

SEALS : THE FIRST TASMANIAN INDUSTRY

Tasmania's first industry was sealing. In 1799 when Bass and Flinders returned to Sydney, after their historic voyage around Tasmania, they reported sighting huge seal colonies on islands and rocks off Tasmania.

The colony of Sydney desparately needed a product which they could trade for food and other goods with visiting ships. So, the Government of New South Wales encouraged sealing in Tasmania. Seal-oil was used back in those days for household lighting and for use in industry. Their fur was also an important part of the skin trade.

Sealers were a wild and hardy group of men who lived in harsh and filthy conditions on the islands. They kidnapped aboriginal women and kept them as wives and workers.

The aboriginal women were excellent swimmers and hunters. They would swim out to rocks where seals were basking in the sun. Pretending to be seals they would crawl slowly up to a seal and then club it to death.

Originally there were three types of seal around Tasmania, the Elephant Seal, the Leopard Seal and the Fur Seal but the sealers were greedy and had no idea of conservation. They went on killing the seals until they were almost extinct and so the industry stopped.

Today, around Tasmania, only the fur seal survives. Their numbers are slowly increasing.

BEACHCOMBING

Being an island, Tasmania is edged with many fine beaches and rugged headlands. Because of this, you will probably find yourself walking along a beach, at some time during your holiday.

Here are some drawings, of just a few of the things you might find, if you go beachcombing.

Don't forget to keep a lookout for Aboriginal Middens - remember not to remove any shells from them.

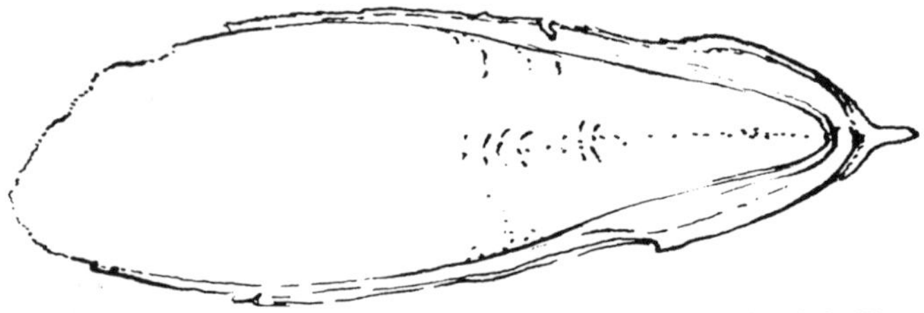

Cuttlebone (The "backbone" of a Cuttlefish which is like a squid)

Cowrie
(only small ones in Tassie)

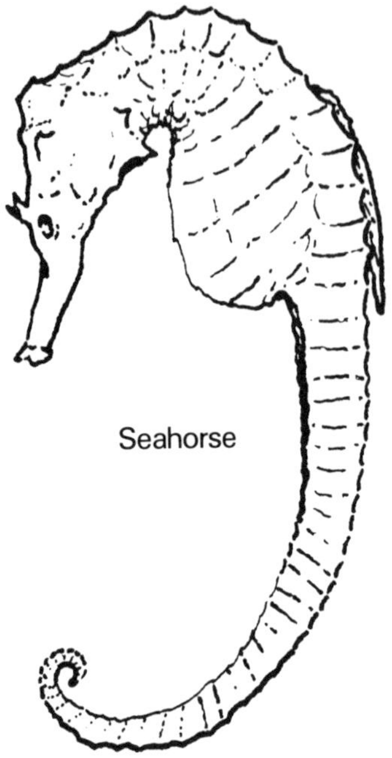

Seahorse

Warrener Shell. (Common in Aboriginal middens. Green and light-green to white.)

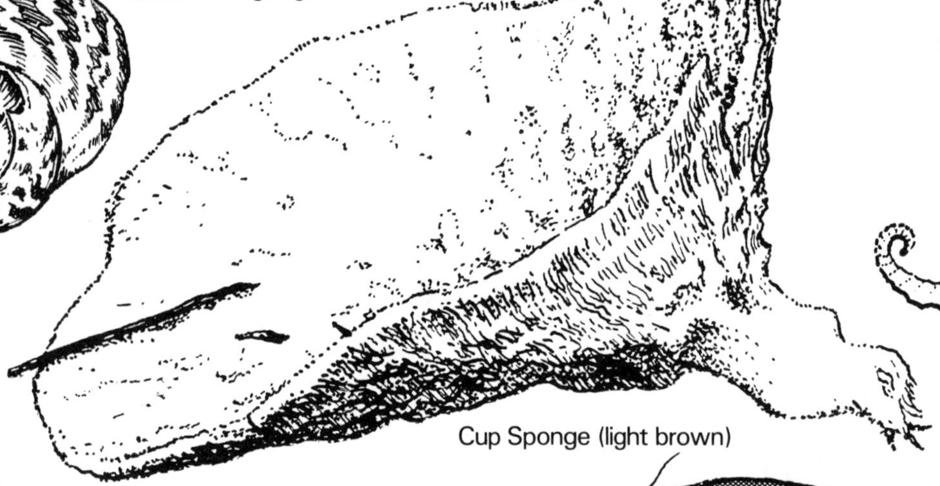

Cup Sponge (light brown)

Trochus Shell (pink)

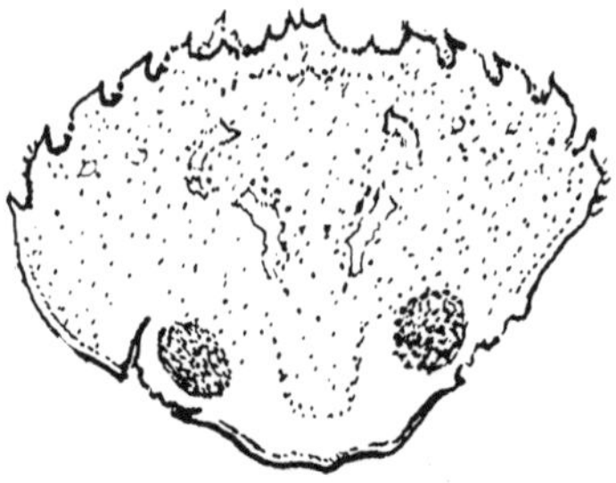

Surf Crab (two red spots)

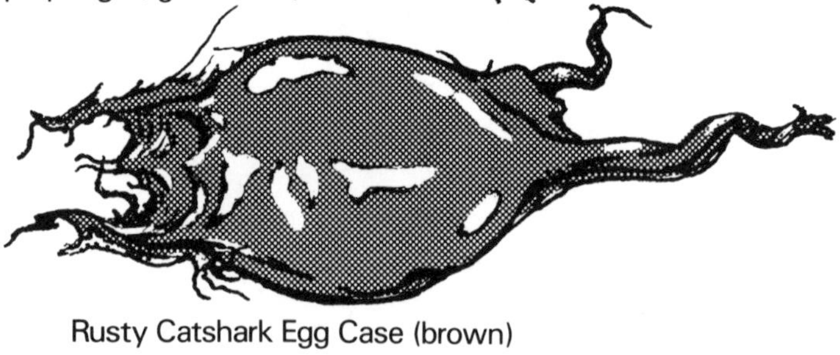

Rusty Catshark Egg Case (brown)

Spindle Shell (white)

Lace Bryozoan (white)

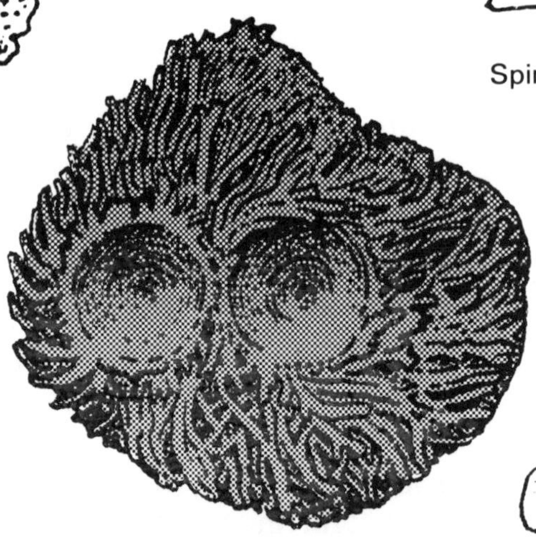

The "root" of Bull Kelp (brown)

Coral (There are other corals around Tasmania but the sea usually breaks them. White)

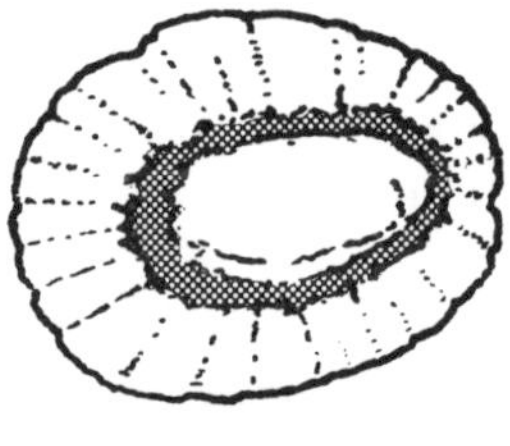

Common Limpet

Razor Shell or Chinamans Fingernail (pink)

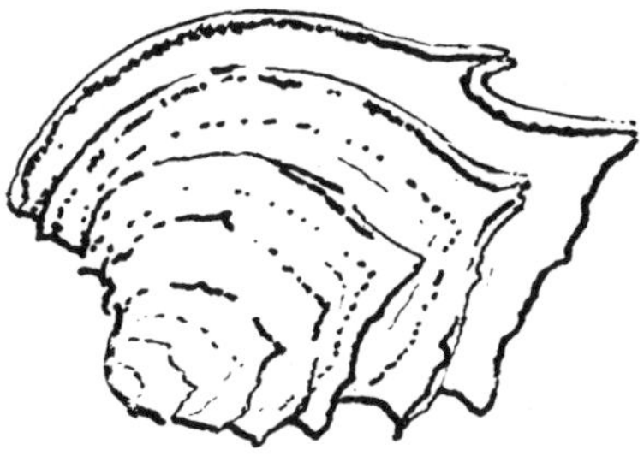

Frilled Venerid or Wedding Cake Venus
(white)

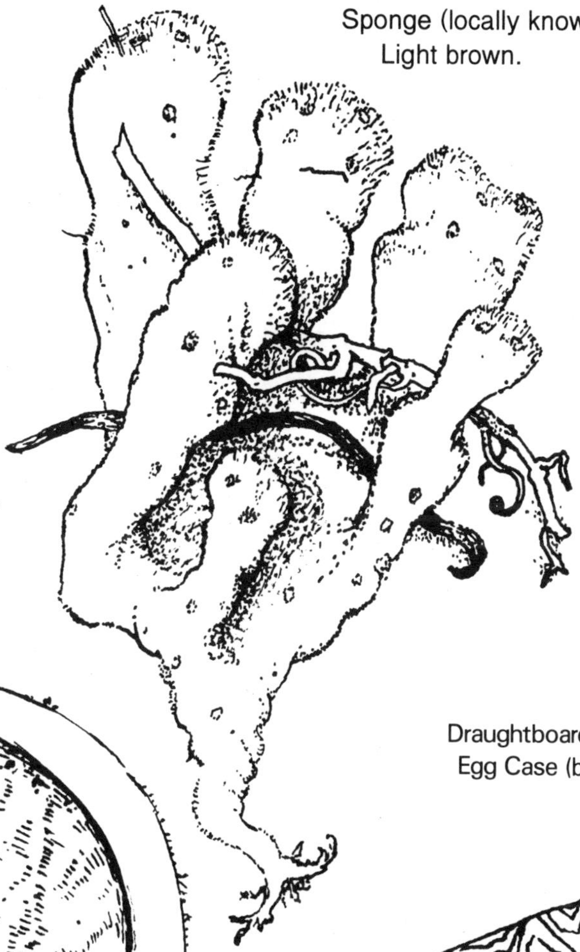

Sponge (locally known as Dead Man's Fingers.
Light brown.

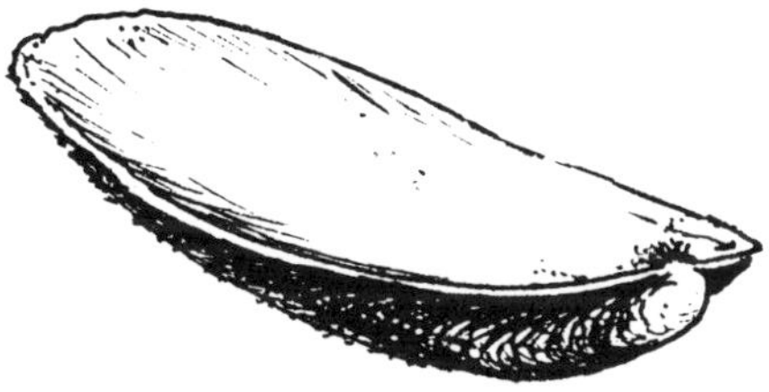

Blue Mussel Shell
(Edible shellfish)

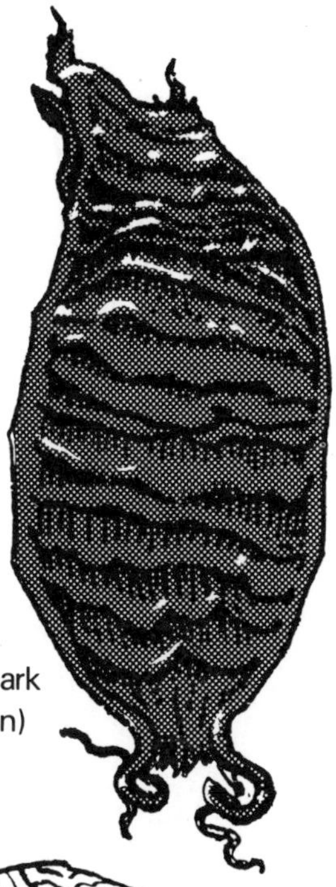

Draughtboard Shark
Egg Case (brown)

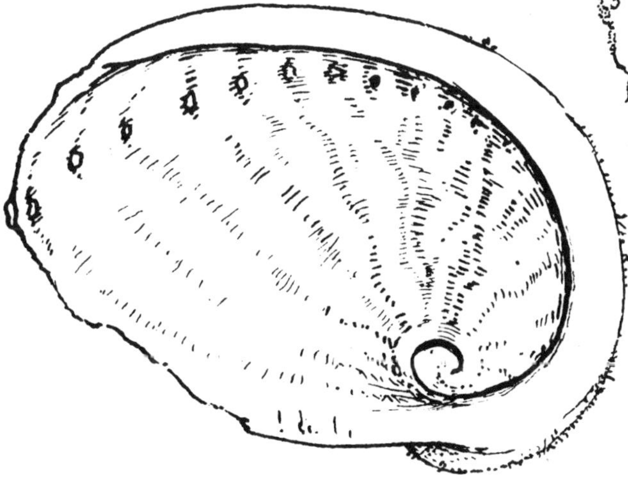

Abalone (Edible shellfish. Divers make a lot of money gathering these. Can you draw the pretty Mother-of-Pearl colours inside the shell?)

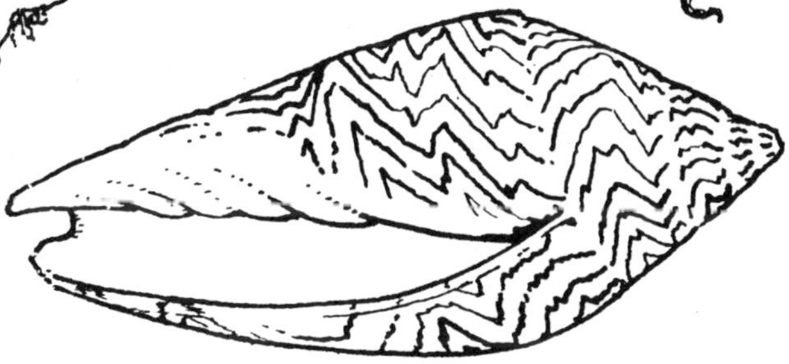

Wavy Volute (orange with brown stripes)

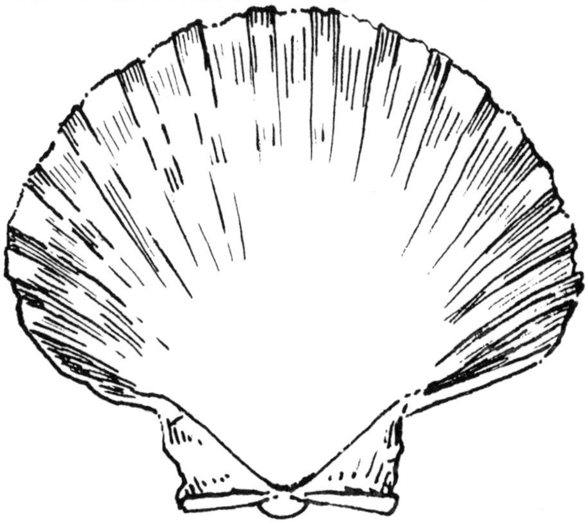

Tasmanian Scallop (Edible shellfish. The shells have different halves, one cupped, the other flat. Pink to orange.)

Use this space to draw some of the things you find.
Do you know what they are?

POWER FROM WATER?

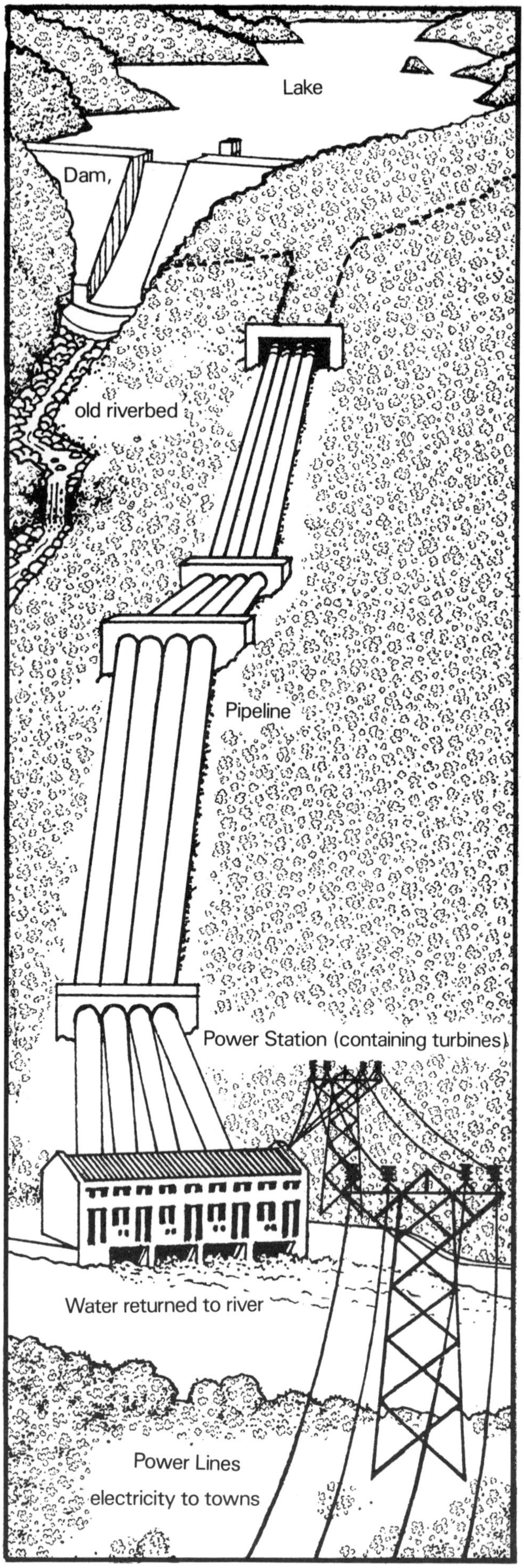

How do you turn water into electricity? Well, if you've ever stood under a waterfall or been swimming in the surf you'll know just how strong flowing water can be. But, to turn that power into electricity the water must be harnessed.

To do that a dam must be built and the water channelled off into a tunnel or pipe. Usually the pipe runs down a hill to make the water flow even faster. At the bottom of the pipe a turbine and generator are placed. A turbine is like a huge propeller. As the water passes through, the turbine spins, this in turn rotates the generator. The generator is made of magnets and copper plates or coiled wire. When the magnet spins around inside the copper coil it produces electricity.

Hydro-Electricity is nothing new to Tasmania. In fact Tasmania was one of the first places in the world to have hydro-electricity. A power station built at Duck Reach provided power to Launceston as long ago as 1895 but it wasn't until 1911 that a really big hydro-electric scheme was planned for the whole state.

The first big power station was at Waddamana, south of the Great Lake. Today there are 27 hydro-electric power stations in Tasmania. They are all located in the wetter, more mountainous parts of the state.

Tasmania is a perfect place for hydro-electric developments because it has mountainous regions some of which receive over 350 centimetres of rain a year.

Until hydro-electric power was developed in Tasmania, the state had to rely on farming, forestry and mining for export. However, since the Hydro-Electric Commission began to sell electricity many big manufacturing companies have moved to Tasmania.

Perhaps you have heard about the protests that occured when the Hydro-Electric Commission wanted to dam the Franklin River in South-West Tasmania.

Some of the points in favour of more hydro-electric developments are:

- Hydro-Electricity provides "clean" power. Coal, oil, and nuclear power are used elsewhere to produce electricity. They produce pollution in the form of heat, smoke and radioactive waste.
- To produce hydro-electricity lakes have been created or enlarged. These can be used for swimming, boating and fishing.

- The dams have been built in what were once remote areas. Roads made to the dams now allow people to drive into areas that could only be visited by walking.
- By providing large amounts of cheap power Tasmania can attract industries which will help create more jobs.

Some of the points against hydro-electric development are:-

- That exisiting lakes, rivers and forests are flooded to create bigger lakes. People can go fishing, boating and swimming in them in their natural state anyway.
- That roads, dams, power stations and pipelines scar and spoil the wilderness areas.
- That whilst the power is "clean" the industries which come here to use the power create pollution.
- That we already have enough power and that building more dams is a waste of money.
- That more tourists will visit Tasmania if the wilderness areas are left untouched by people.

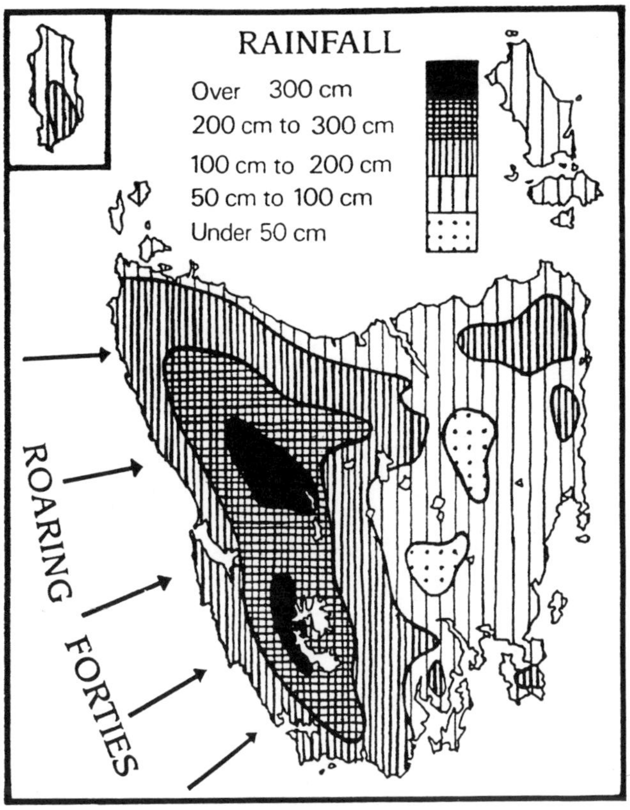

While you are travelling in Tasmania you will probably see some of these hydro-electric developments. There are guided tours at some power stations. By contacting the Hydro-Electric Commission you can find out when and where these are.

This bumper-sticker was seen all over Australia in the early 1980's.

It became the symbol of the first large conservation protest.

RAINFALL

Have you heard of "the roaring forties"? That's the name sailors gave the windy region that runs right around the world between forty and fifty degrees south of the Equator.

Tasmania lies between forty and forty three and a half degrees south of the Equator right in the path of these winds. The winds usually blow from west to east. When these winds reach Tasmania they have travelled thousands of kilometres across oceans picking up moisture along the way. When these moisture laden winds arrive in Tasmania, they are forced over the mountains, as they do the air cools, clouds form and rain falls. Once across the mountains, the air warms up and the sky clears.

That is why the western half of Tasmania receives much more rain and snow than other parts of Australia. It is also why Tasmania has so many rivers, lakes and streams.

Did you know that even though parts of Tasmania have the highest rainfall in Australia — Perth, Melbourne, Sydney, Brisbane and Darwin all receive more rain than Hobart!?

WHERE WE WENT

Where did you go on your holiday? Use this map to keep a record of where you went in Tasmania. Not all of the roads and towns are shown, so feel free to add any extras. You could make up your own symbols and colours for the Key below. For example, I've shown Historic Towns using this symbol *.

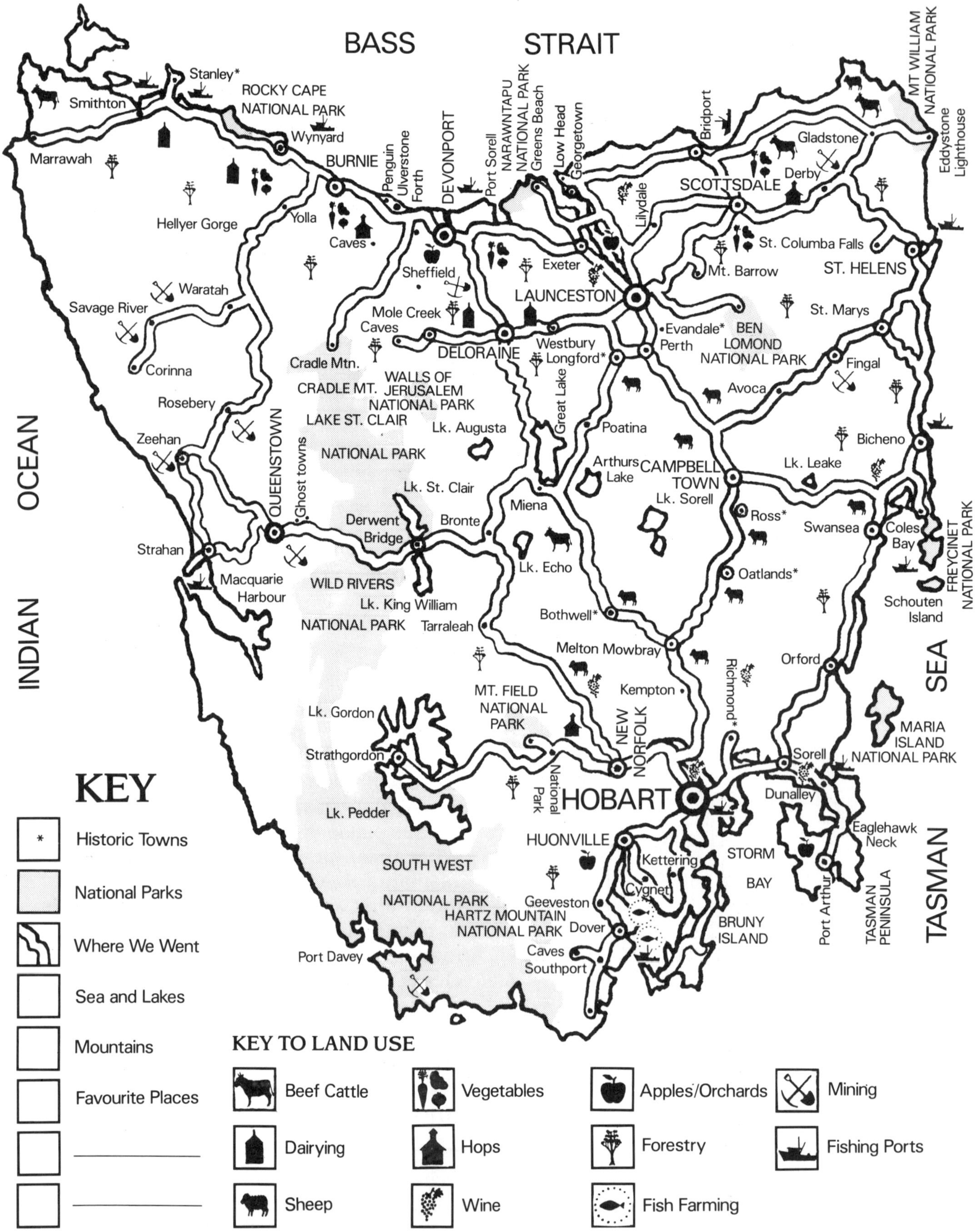

CROSSWORD

CLUES DOWN

1. A rough and fast part of a river or a small waterfall.
2. The _ _ _ is a headland at Stanley.
3. Something you do in water.
4. A drink made from Tasmanian grapes.
5. A wild river in Western Tasmania.
7. A shelter built in the bush.
9. The Stuff left after a fire or a type of tree.
10. Furry, tree climbing animals with long tails.
11. It shines in the sky during the day.
12. A piece of paper with countries and roads printed on it.
13. The early explorer who sailed with Flinders right around Tasmania. He had a Strait named after him.
15. They drill for it in Bass Strait.
18. To get to the top of steep mountains you have to _ _ _ _ _.
19. A stripey Tasmanian animal that is possibly extinct.

The answers are on page 32.

CLUES ACROSS

3. It is white and very cold.
5. Most Tasmanian animals are covered with it.
6. Animals can stratch and dig with it.
7. Tasmania's Capital City.
8. A large wall for holding back water.
10. Possums can be a _ _ _ _ in gardens.
12. A hole where you dig for minerals.
13. The noise sheep make.
14. A plant grown on strings in Tasmania to help make beer.
16. Tasmania used to grow lots of this fruit.
17. A city in northern Tasmania.
20. A winter sport on some Tasmanian mountains.
21. Some people think the wombat looks like a _ _ _ _.

SPOTTO

How many of these shapes can you spot during your travels?

Some things you will see more than once, others you will have to look hard for. Put a tick beside each one as you spot it. You might like to name the shapes and draw an arrow to the spot on the map where you saw it.

Don't be disappointed if you can't spot them all. Tassie may only be a small island but it is still hard to visit everywhere in one holiday.

Add up your score at the end of your holiday. The answers are on page 52. Try not to peek.

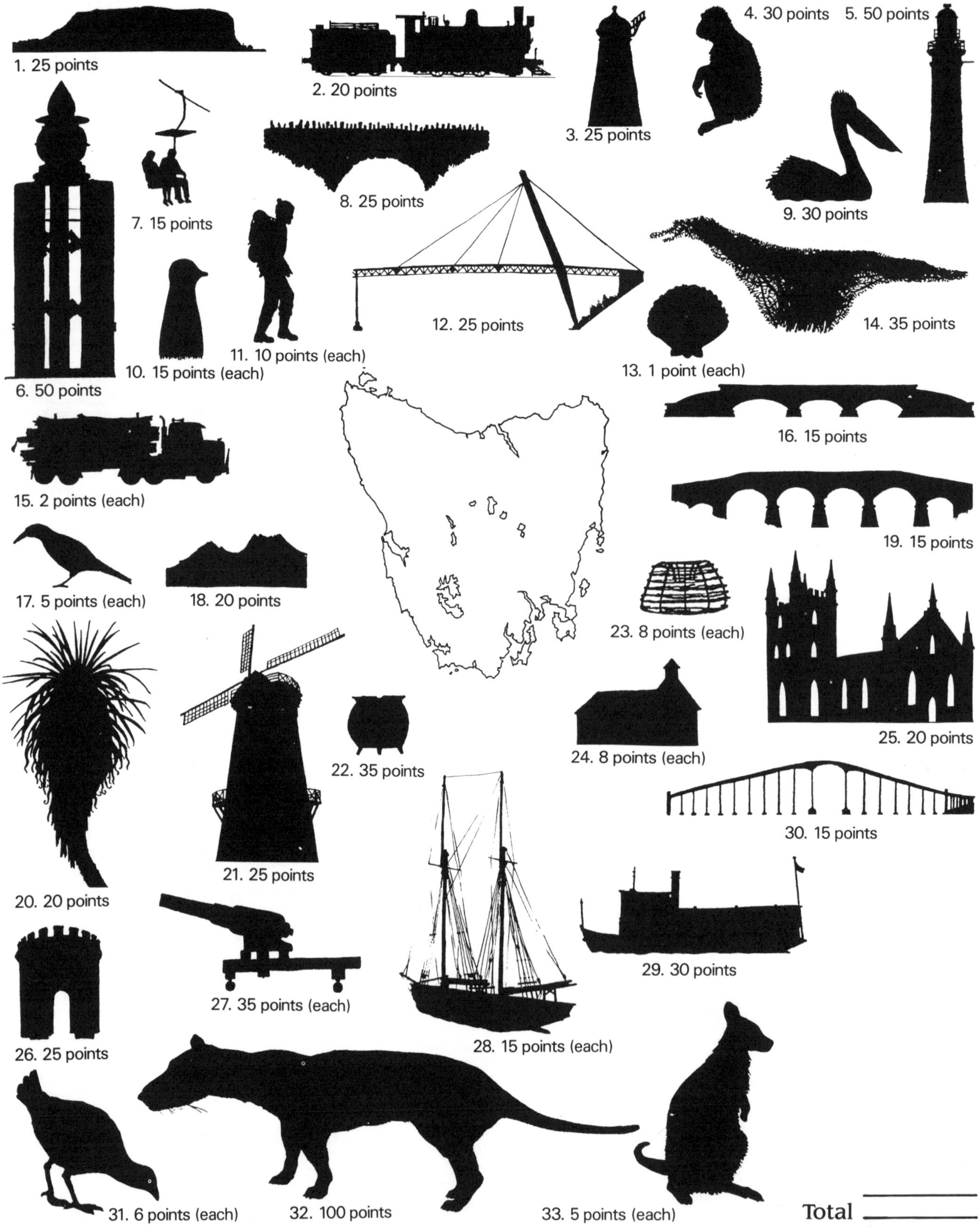

Total ____________

MY DIARY,

Many early explorers and settlers in Tasmania kept a diary. From those diaries we can find out what life was like back then.

Keep your own diary by writing about what you see or do each day. At the end of your holiday you will have your own story of Tasmanian Adventures.

Day 1

Day 2

Day 3

SPOTTO ANSWERS

1. The Nut at Stanley. 2. There are trains at Perth, Deloraine, Don and Stanley (you might have found more). 3. Callington Mill, Oatlands. 4. Monkeys in City Park, Launceston. 5. Eddystone Lighthouse (not the Shot Tower). 6. War Memorial, Ulverstone. 7. Chairlift in The Gorge, Launceston. 8. Spiky Bridge near Swansea. 9. Yes, there are Pelicans in Tassie, along the coast. 10. Garbage Bins, Penguin. 11. Bushwalker. 12. Batman Bridge. 13. Tasmanian Scallop Shell. 14. Crocodile Hedge near Oatlands. 15. Log trucks, everywhere. 16. Ross Bridge. 17. Mountain Currawong. 18. Cradle Mountain. 19. Richmond Bridge. 20. Pandani (west coast or mountain forests). 21. Windmill, Launceston. 22. Trypot for boiling down Whale blubber, Salamanca Place. 23. Craypot, used to catch Crayfish. 24. Oast House, anywhere near New Norfolk. 25. Ruined Church at Port Arthur. 26. Guard House, Port Arthur. 27. Cannon, Kangaroo Bluff, Bellerive. 28. There are a few Tall Ships around Tassie. You might have spotted the "May Queen" in Hobart, "The Defender" in Launceston or the "Enterprise" at Bicheno. 29. The Derwent Ferry "Emmalisa". 30. The Tasman Bridge, Hobart. Part of it was knocked down by a ship in 1975. 31. Tasmania's "Roadrunner", the Native Hen. 32. This is a tricky one! Did you see a real Tassie Tiger or the one's in the Museum in Hobart or Launceston - congratulations if you did. 33. Bennett's Wallaby. Did you get to pat one?

Day 4

Day 5

Day 6

Day 7